INQUIRY AND DECISION

INQUIRY
AND DECISION

A Methodology for Management
and the Social Sciences

John O'Shaughnessy

Associate Professor in Business
Graduate School of Business, Columbia University, New York

BOOKS
10 East 53d St., New York 10022
(a division of Harper & Row Publishers, Inc.)

Published in the U.S.A. 1973 by:

HARPER & ROW PUBLISHERS, INC.
BARNES & NOBLE IMPORT DIVISION

ISBN 06-495310-6

Printed in Great Britain

Preface

Decision-making is a major focus of attention in the social sciences. This is not surprising since it is through the process of decision that problems are solved and action is taken. A study of how people actually do make decisions, given their predispositions and perceptions, is important for predicting behaviour while a study of how people should make decisions, given a set of goals and choices, is important because we hope that such studies will make the probability of fulfilling the goal as high as possible.

A major problem lies in determining the elements of decision. This book concentrates on the logical processes involved and uses these processes as a way of integrating the methodological contributions of those social science disciplines that seem most relevant to the decision-maker who is concerned with choices involving courses of action. As long as the bulk of management problems remain uncharted, the ability to 'think out' a decision must remain an important aid to effective decision. If the manager seeks to choose the 'best' alternative in the circumstances, he needs first to decide how he should understand what is going on, given the forces at work.

This book is designed to help the decision-maker avoid some of the errors of a logical nature that can arise in moving from a set of stated goals to the selection of a course of action that satisfies these goals. It is argued that the steps in such decision-making—establishing objectives, identifying alternatives, discovering consequences and finally choice—are composed of the elements of description, explanation, prediction, and evaluation about which much is known that could help to make decisions more effective. Although most of the examples chosen to illustrate the text are taken from management, this should not unduly limit its usefulness in other areas since many of the decisions made by the manager have strong similarities to those made in every field of endeavour.

I would like to acknowledge the help of colleagues in the writing of this book. It was through discussions with Professor David Miller that the idea of the book arose in the first place. His immense knowledge of management science was always readily available and his help and encouragement are gratefully acknowledged. Other colleagues at Columbia who read through drafts of the manuscripts and offered valuable suggestions were Professors Martin Starr, Margaret Chandler, William Newman and Frenck Waage. Former colleagues Tom Cass, Harry Ward and Michael Godfrey gave very helpful advice, while Morris Holbrook, a Ph.D. student at Columbia, made some valuable criticism. A special debt is due to Professor Ernest Nagel. His comments and discussion with me of the text helped me avoid a number of substantive errors. My early interest in the Philosophy of Science was aroused by his writings and he has influenced the thinking in this book more than any other writer. I am deeply grateful.

I am indebted to Holt, Rinehart & Winston, Inc. for permission to reproduce an illustration.

Finally, acknowledgment of a debt to my wife Marjorie without whose help there would have been no book, and to my son Nicholas who helped eliminate so many of my literary inelegancies.

Contents

Chapter 1

INTRODUCTION

We all make decisions and many of these decisions involve selecting what we believe to be the best of several possible courses of action. Of course, the 'best' course of action depends on what we are trying to do; what needs or objectives we are trying to meet. All such 'prescriptive' decision-making presupposes that we have some goal, need or objective which we wish to satisfy. If the wrong objective is set, a course of action is likely to be chosen that does not relate to real needs and this may be worse than choosing a second-rate means for attaining true objectives. A businessman who sets as his aim merely an increase in the volume of sales may achieve the objective by adopting pricing policies that could lead to bank-ruptcy; far better that he adopt any means that at least maintains profitability.

In many decisions, the courses of action required to meet objectives are known and well established. We have no difficulty in knowing the course of action to take if our objective is merely to get to work. But the decisions that concern us are not this easy. The best course of action depends not only on what we want to achieve but also on the situation. Yet events occur that change the situation so that current courses of action to meet objectives may no longer be suit-able. Thus, current marketing strategies may be inappropriate if the situation in the market is changed by the activities of competitors.

It often happens that the events or forces that have brought about the changes of interest are not obvious but have to be identified. Thus, when a car breaks down, a change is observed but it is still necessary to discover what went wrong, that is, what events occurred that resulted in the breakdown. Similarly, if the manager observes an increase in labour grievances, he seeks the reasons. In other words, changes in a situation that are perceived as likely to affect objectives may need to be explained and the resulting explanation used as a guide in the research for appropriate courses of action.

13

The problem of understanding some change that has occurred is often a necessary preliminary to knowing what to do about it. The first step to such understanding is to examine the change and attempt to classify it according to the system of knowledge wherein a solution may lie. In the examples above, the car breakdown might be classified as an electrical problem and the increase in labour grievances as a problem in industrial relations.

As we classify a problem, we hypothesize as to the nature of a solution. Thus, if a fall-off in sales is classified as a problem in salesman motivation, we have hypothesized a relationship between the fall-off in sales and some change in salesman motivation. Such hypotheses require testing. If the manager acts on the assumption that it is a motivation problem when, in reality, competitive activity is the reason, he has acted on an unjustified assumption, and has incorrectly diagnosed the problem.

On the above argument, one cannot begin to attack a problem without first having some idea of a solution. Northrop has argued differently. He claims that analysis of the problem precedes the formulation of hypotheses regarding possible solutions.[1] 'It is the problem and its characteristics as revealed by analysis which guides one first to the relevant facts and then, once the relevant facts are known, to the relevant hypotheses.' But analysis of a problem and hypothesis about a problem cannot be so easily separated. As Patrick Gardiner points out, though the reference was not to Northrop:

> 'For his dictum suggests, amongst other things, that the finding out what happened and the finding out why it happened are two distinct procedures. And this is not the case. It is incorrect to speak of "finding out the facts" as if this were a process separate from, and prior to, the discovery of causal relations: there is what may be called a *procedural interconnection* between the two.'[2]

Although a solution may be only vaguely conceived, it guides the selection of relevant information.

Even when the problem of understanding has been 'solved', the manager needs the experience or creativity to set up courses of

[1] F. S. C. Northrop, *The Logic of the Sciences and the Humanities*, Meridian Books, The World Publishing Co., New York, 1959, p. 17.
[2] Patrick Gardiner, *The Nature of Historical Explanation*, Oxford University Press, London, 1968, p. 78.

14

action suggested by the problem solution. He has the further step of predicting the likely consequences stemming from the alternatives and evaluating these consequences in order to choose the one most likely to achieve objectives.

DECISION CLASSIFICATION

Every problem is made up of the categories of description, explanation, prediction, evaluation and prescription, and for each of these categories rational methods have been developed that could help in the solution of unstructured problems. These categories are basically those of the philosopher John Dewey, who regarded logic as essentially an approach to inquiry, and inquiry as a process by which uncertainty is reduced. Charles Morris, in the field of semiotic, has pointed out that inquiry covers designative problems (description, explanation and prediction) and problems which are appraisive in essence as well as those that are prescriptive.[1] He argues that only designative problems are, in principle, value-free and so they have greater claim to be the subject matter of science. Eugene Meehan, in emphasizing the importance of these processes of inquiry, argues that every prescriptive decision presupposes description and explanation.[2]

Description

Whenever a person relates what he has seen or heard, he makes a decision. From a whole range of possible aspects and interpretations, he makes a selection. Such selection introduces the possibility of bias. Since all knowledge depends on observation, and progress in knowledge on communication, the value of any specific knowledge rests ultimately on the value of the underlying observation, testimony, or 'protocol statements' which record details of the observations made.

Explanation

According to Nagel, explanation consists of describing the conditions under which the event to be explained varies, fits into some known

[1] Charles Morris, *Signification and Significance*, M.I.T. Press, Cambridge, Mass., 1964, p. 27.
[2] Eugene J. Meehan, *Value Judgment and Social Science*, The Dorsey Press, Homewood, Illinois, 1969.

15

system, or follows from some principle accepted as true. This may take the form of showing cause, origins, effects, purpose or function. Although description and classification reveal features, resemblances and differences, they are not generally regarded as explanation since they do not point out why or how these come about.

An explanation should not only account for the facts to be explained but should also be intelligible, in that it makes sense in terms of other known truths. Finally, it should survive testing and so be supported by the evidence designed to test it. There are many types of explanation, and the one selected will depend on the purpose of the inquiry. Thus, simply to ask 'Why?' in itself begs the question as to the type of explanation that is appropriate. For example, if we were to ask why there is a strike, there are a whole number of possible answers—actions that could have been taken to prevent it; motives of those striking; how the strike evolved; purpose of the strike; the role the strike plays in power politics, and so on. On these grounds Fischer suggests that for serious inquiry, 'Why?' should be consigned to the 'semantical rubbish heap'.[1]

Prediction

A prediction makes statements about some future state of affairs as an inference from the state of past or current events. Although much prediction is based on explanation, there can be prediction without explanation.

Evaluation

In an evaluative decision, the decision-maker determines the relative worth of some person, alternative or thing. Every evaluation presupposes some objective, as from this objective stems the criterion used to rank the items being evaluated.

Prescription

A prescriptive decision involves the selection of a course of action. Decision-making is often regarded as invariably this process, though if one chooses a particular explanation it is still a decision and not a selection of a course of action. Decision alternatives need not be restricted to courses of action.

In general, it is functions at the operational level in a business that supply descriptive data, while the research function usually

[1] D. H. Fischer, *Historians' Fallacies*, Harper & Row, New York, 1970.

16

supplies information that is explanatory and predictive; the control function being largely evaluative and the planning function mainly prescriptive.

In the chapters that follow, this book discusses the logical processes of description, explanation, prediction and evaluation. It also describes the stages in the prescriptive decision. It will be argued in the last chapter that the logical processes of description, explanation, prediction and evaluation are essential elements in the prescriptive decision. Different stages in the prescriptive decision can be composed of a different mix of logical processes; they do not necessarily follow as a set sequence, as may be suggested by their treatment in this book.

Chapter 2

DESCRIPTIVE DECISION

A descriptive decision manifests itself in a descriptive statement. Such statements, for example, would be descriptions of processes and procedures. They are commonly regarded as factual statements because they are based on simple direct observation where no attempt is made to change what is being observed. Yet observation can be erroneous. For it is selective and depends on interpretation of sensory stimuli transmitted to the brain via the sense organs. Such interpretation involves giving meaning to sensations by organizing them via concepts and theory.

Selectivity of observation

All observation is selective. We perceive only a very small part of what is perceptible. Our selection is determined not only by the intensity, novelty and complexity of the stimuli, but also by what we believe to be relevant to our requirements. This in turn demands that we have some idea about how our needs can be satisfied, or how the problem giving rise to the need can be solved. The industrial engineer who is examining low labour output will attend to work flow, feedback on performance to the operator, work methods, financial incentives, and so on; the industrial psychologist may check selection techniques and working conditions; while the social psychologist will seek to discover work-group norms and supervisory behaviour patterns. It is known that residents in a district are normally ignorant of such things as the names of local streets or town officials unless they have had occasion to need such knowledge.[1] (On this basis it seems surprising—if we are to believe the films—that those training spies feel it necessary to teach the prospective spy such details about the town where he is supposed to have lived. A

[1] George Bernard Shaw once wrote: 'If you wish to be thoroughly misinformed about a place, ask a man who has lived the best thirty years of his life there.'

18

suspected spy who shows such uncommon knowledge may in fact be revealing his guilt!)

Efficient observation is that which contributes to the attainment of goals with economy of effort. The value of observation depends on the relevance of the criterion used to guide the observer. This, as we have seen, depends on the extent to which goals and problems are correctly identified, and on the development of sensitivity towards the factors relevant to a solution. One aim of training is to increase sensitivity in finding factors previously treated as irrelevant or entirely overlooked.

How much we observe partly depends on our purposes. It may be more appropriate to sacrifice details to obtain a general view. Also, *when* we observe may be relevant to the value of the observations, since conditions may affect their accuracy.

SENSATION, INTERPRETATION AND PERCEPTION

Sensation is the reception of a stimulus by a sense organ. But an individual is not just a passive receiver of data from the outside world. We seldom experience sensation without automatically interpreting it, though the particular combination of pure sensation and interpretation will vary with the situation.[1] Interpretation can be distinguished from inference. An interpretation is a conclusion reached through giving meaning to sensation without any explicit marshalling of evidence, whereas an inference is a conclusion based on factors which can be explicitly given as evidence in its support. Not every philosopher would accept this distinction between interpretation and inference; Blanshard, for example, regards the distinction as simply being one between implicit and explicit inference.

Perception embraces both selection and interpretation of sensory stimuli. In perception a person relates the sensation to other things with which he is familiar; that is, he classifies the various elements in the situation to form a pattern that is meaningful in terms of his past experience. This at least is the theory: we are not aware of receiving sensations, but only of our own perceptions. However, on the basis of this theory, the belief that there are sensations that

---

[1] Phenomenology claims a method for getting 'back to the things themselves', i.e. to a description of the given without any bias stemming from our purposes or preconceptions.

register the same in every observer's mind is erroneous. Only a common background of shared experience leads to an overlap in perceptions.

A car would not be classified as such by a person who had never seen or heard of one before. Similarly, many common consumer products in one country would go unrecognized elsewhere and one 'would not know what to make of them'. As Doby points out: 'If a physician who lived in the eighteenth century were to be returned to life today and asked to peer through an electron microscope at a slide containing viruses, would he see the same things the contemporary physician sees? The answer is no.'[1] Doby then argues how the process of observation is dependent on concepts and theories held by the observer: 'The conceptual framework from which one views data not only determines what one sees in a scientific sense, but what one does not see as well.'

The discovery and measurement of the way in which people perceive some object or event is of great interest to social scientists. Market structure analysis is a market-research technique for segmenting markets on the basis of consumer perceptions. The technique, as developed by Volney Stefflre, makes the assumption that people will behave similarly towards objects which they describe as alike, since similarity of description suggests similarity of perception. There is evidence for this, as it has been found that products which are described as most alike are those which are most freely substituted for each other. When people judge products on a number of dimensions, the problem arises of making comparisons between the summated judgments. The technique, for showing the resulting configurations to allow for comparisons, is the statistical technique of multidimensional scaling. Market structure analysis, though in its infancy (embodying as it does a number of dubious assumptions), has been used to position a company's products vis-à-vis other brands, and to build new ones based on consumer perceptions of their ideal product.

Since an observational statement is a description, errors in perception became errors in observation and description. One type of error is due to anticipation of the behaviour or intent of those being observed. Thus, industrial engineers recommend making an instant

[1] J. T. Doby, 'Logic and Levels of Scientific Explanation' in *Sociological Methodology* 1969, ed. E. F. Borgatta, Jossey-Bass, San Francisco, 1969, pp. 139–40.

decision in categorizing activities during random observation study, to avoid bias in interpretation resulting from an observer's anticipating a subject's next activity. If what we see or hear resembles what we want or expect in terms of our experiences and needs, we tend to interpret in these terms. That which we do not want nor expect to see or hear, we may ignore or reject. An interviewer, after reading an applicant's résumé, can develop expectations which, through selective perception, appear to be confirmed during the interview. This is more particularly so the more ambiguous the original stimulus. In the absence of the obviously relevant, the irrelevant is often used to reach conclusions. This is especially so in assessing personality traits—a person may be judged to lack drive purely on the basis of the speed of his movements. Thouless amusingly quotes C. E. Montague:

'A supporter of Cambridge, looking at a photograph of the Oxford cricket eleven is reported by C. E. Montague to have said: "Look at them! The hang-dog expressions! The narrow, ill-set mongol eyes! The thin, cruel lips! Prejudice apart, would you like to meet that gang in a quiet place on a dark night?" '[1]

Thus, while observation depends on experience, the latter occupies the mind by presupposition giving rise to unconscious bias in perception. Whether a man is repairing, setting up, maintaining or dismantling a machine, can only be determined from knowledge based on experience; it is easy for the inexperienced to be misled.

A person's emotional state also influences his capacity for making objective observations. A manager may have difficulty in discovering the reasons for some dispute because the emotionally excited participants may give inconsistent accounts of the events, and because he himself may be emotionally involved.

How do we test our own observations and those of others for reliability? Testimony is particularly important since much of our knowledge is based on observations made by others. The main test is corroboration of witnesses with no motive for lying. General agreement suggests objectivity in the sense that the observations are unbiased except for bias common to all the observers. A so-called fact becomes so only by general agreement that it is true beyond question, though such belief may be unwarranted. Other

[1] R. H. Thouless, *Straight and Crooked Thinking*, Pan Books Ltd, London, 1956, p. 135.

considerations besides that of corroboration are: whether the physical conditions were conducive to accurate observation; whether the observer had the necessary sensory acuity; whether the selection and interpretation was likely to be biased by lack of experience or emotional involvement; and finally, whether the events were sufficiently recent or important to be remembered.

Records that embody past observations may be consulted for data relevant to a problem. For example, a firm's budgets can be used to indicate expenditure on various activities, to avoid wasting time examining those which offer little scope for economy. A firm's sales records may be a source of data in market research, e.g. sales in geographic divisions, size of orders, size of customers, trends and seasonal fluctuations. There may be difficulty in checking the validity of records. Thus, the data from library research for market research is often difficult to check, as it depends on trade publications and magazine articles whose collection methods may not be open to public scrutiny.

CLASSIFICATION

Perception involves classification, while description itself classifies the perceptions and forms them into a pattern through the use of concepts. It was said earlier that in interpreting sensation a person relates the sensation to other things. He also abstracts common features from a number of objects or situations to arrive at concepts, whether these are as mundane as 'whiteness', or as devised as 'optimization', 'product life cycle,' 'operator performance,' and so on. The word 'construct' is sometimes used for concept when the concept is part of a scientific vocabulary. A class is a concept, so that effective classification ultimately depends on having the right concepts for the purpose. This in turn depends on having the right perceptual experiences to form the basis for learning. As Alice Mary Hilton comments:

> 'We learn the concept of number by counting, the concept of shape by fitting objects together, the concept of quality by comparing values, the concept of rules of conduct by observing (and judging) the evidence of good or bad behaviour. We learn an algebraic formula by seeing several examples and observing their common formal property.

22

Yet we cannot understand the concepts of number, or shape, or quality, or rules of conduct or an algebraic formula without the ability to abstract the common form from the instance we have observed.'[1]

The development of useful concepts is the groundwork of any subject, e.g. the concept of cost as displaced alternatives in economics. Major advances have been made in a subject merely by introducing new concepts on how to classify or relate things rather than through major discoveries.

Any descriptive word classifies. All common nouns by which a person describes his perceptions are classes into which he places them. We are more likely to perceive things we can classify, not those for which we have no labels. The extent to which a classification is crude and general determines the extent to which we are sensitive to differences. Thus, a person ignorant of a car engine notices less than a mechanic when the car bonnet is lifted. Similarly, the human engineering specialist, taught the concept of 'blind positioning movements', is much more likely to observe such movements than those who have no label for such movements. One of the aims in marketing is to teach consumers to make fine sub-divisions within some product class (e.g. coffee) on the basis of differences that help the manufacturer to sell his product.

By classifying some object consistently in one way, there arises a difficulty in classifying it in another. A chief executive may classify his shareholders on the basis of the type of dividend paid, but may forget that sometimes they can also be classified as the most likely prospective customers for his product.

In logic the process of breaking down a class (or genus) into sub-classes (categories or species) is referred to as 'logical division'. The term 'classification' is reserved for the grouping of entities into classes, and of these into wider ones.

Logical Division

Whenever we select a class and break it down into sub-classes, the process is one of logical division. Division presupposes a class. Customers can be divided on a socio-economic basis (or some other attribute), but a divided individual unit (such as in drawing up a

[1] Alice Mary Hilton, *Logic, Computing Machines and Automation*, Meridian Books, The World Publishing Co., New York, 1966, p. 72.

company organization chart) does not constitute logical division. Division must also be distinguished from conceptual analysis, which is the mere listing of attributes. For example, the listing of the attributes of a product is not division, though each one might form the basis for a division of markets as happens in market segmentation.

Classification is the complementary but reverse process to logical division. The difference lies in viewpoint and the starting-point in procedure. Thus, if we take a mass of customers and separate them into socio-economic groups, we carry out logical division; but if we put individual customers into their appropriate groups, we classify them.

There may be a problem in determining the appropriate genus or class to break down. For in segmenting a market the first problem is to define the generic need for which the company caters before setting out the more specific market needs it aims to satisfy. This generic need defines the sphere of competition, and avoids commitment to a market segment without consideration of the other possibilities available. Levitt points out that the film industry did not recognize that it catered for the generic need for entertainment, and that its competition was likely to come from television.[1] 'It thought it was in the movie business when it was actually in the entertainment business.' But Levitt does not state how this genus was considered in defining the firm's competition. If we look at Fig. 1, we see that Levitt had many other possibilities.

As a guide to competition, the entertainment need is debatable since a more generic need is the occupation of leisure time. And both may be too wide for guiding the individual firm to the wider range of alternatives. Thus the selection of the relevant 'summum' genus depends on purpose and requires judgment in evaluating alternatives, yet a statement of purpose is seldom so precise that it points to the unique answer.

Classification as an Aid to Discovery

The objectives of classification are not only to facilitate reference but also to aid understanding. The items within a class often have far more in common than is revealed by the criterion used to group

[1] Theodore Levitt, 'Marketing Myopia' in *Modern Marketing Strategy*, eds. Edward C. Bursk and John F. Chapman, Harvard University Press, Cambridge, Mass., 1964, pp. 24–48.

them. Darwin, for example, saw in the classification system of Linnaeus evidence for the theory of common descent. In fact, the original classification may have as its main purpose the discovery of more profound similarities among the items within each class. Hence we may classify buyers as heavy users, medium users, etc. of a product to discover the characteristics they have in common as an aid to the development of market strategy.

Basis for Classification
The basis used depends on the purpose of the classification; that

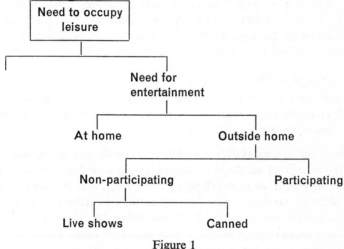

Figure 1

which is most relevant to this purpose depends not on logic but on substantive knowledge. Thus increasing knowledge of consumer buying behaviour leads to new bases for segmenting markets, preferable to the traditional basis of demographic and socio-economic factors (though obtaining operational measures when segments are based on behavioural criteria has a limiting effect). Even in a dichotomous division—where a class is divided into a sub-class and its contradictory (e.g. *X* and not *X*)—the process is formal while the basis of division is not, for the establishment of a positive sub-class in each sub-division depends on substantive know-ledge. But it remains weak, in that the negative term remains unidentified and may not even exist.

25

This is not to suggest that advice can never be given on obtaining a relevant basis for classification in connection with some specific problem. Lazarsfeld refers to approaches listed by Zeisel, and discusses a procedure for classifying reasons given at interviews for buying a particular product. He suggests that the scheme of classification should match 'the actual processes involved in buying and using the product', since 'these are the processes from which the respondent herself has derived her comments; the classification, so to speak, puts the comments back where they come from'. Hence the procedure for establishing the classification is 'to visualize the concrete processes and activities implied by the responses'.[1] Although this classification would certainly help in categorizing responses, it may not be one that meets every need in market research concerning reasons for buying. We may also wish the classification to agree with one derived from psychological theory.

Classification Rules

Though there are no methods for arriving at an ideal classification in all circumstances, there are rules for judging its logic, although these are not always applicable.

1. Each act of logical division should have only one basis, and each step in further subdivision should have a new basis. A violation of this rule leads to overlapping sub-classes, and is known as the fallacy of cross-division. Thus it could be misleading to group those who use product *XYZ* according to whether they are heavy users or upper class; a user might be both. These are two separate bases for a division; one is on the basis of amount bought and the other is a socio-economic basis. It is necessary to keep them separate to avoid overlapping classes. A more important example is the division of 'occupations' in government statistics which mix up 'skills' and 'tasks'; a division on the basic skills would lead to fewer categories and be more useful for the purpose of manpower planning.

   Overlapping classes occur in multiple coding. Thus buyer behaviour may be classified simultaneously as 'voicing disagreement' and 'exhibiting dominance'. Theoretically, such a double classification of the same phenomena can be avoided by setting

[1] Paul F. Lazarsfeld and Morris Rosenberg (eds), *The Language of Social Research*, The Free Press, New York, and Collier-Macmillan Ltd, London, 1955, pp. 88–9.

up a hierarchical classification so that, for instance, 'voicing disagreement' is split into 'exhibiting dominance' and 'not exhibiting dominance'. The rule does not exclude cross-classifications but simply demands that each item must come under one heading.

2. The sub-classes or categories should provide one place and one place only for each item in the class being divided; that is, the categories should be exhaustive as well as mutually exclusive. In the example above there may be buyers of product XYZ who do not use the product for either purpose A or B. Other categories might need to be provided.

A particular problem lies in determining the number of groups into which we classify. If we have too few groups, the richness of the data might be lost, but too many groups are cumbersome.

Nomenclature and Terminology

The system of names given to each sub-class is its nomenclature. But terminology is simply the collection of terms used to describe individual objects or processes. A good nomenclature suggests the relations between classes. Thus, in biology the higher classes have distinct names, and the sub-classes are distinguished by adding a distinctive attribute to the genus. In chemistry, names indicate relationships by modification of their form.

Outside the scientific field, the names given to classes tend to reflect attitude as well as purpose, and different attitudes give rise to different classifications (and vice versa); a classification of 'employees' into 'staff' and 'hourly paid' encourages attitudes of 'them' and 'us'. Similarly, 'material loss' and 'scrap' may refer to the same object but conjure up different attitudes.

SET THEORY

The concept of a class is basic to all problem-solving, since primarily we are dealing with relationships between classes as we generalize and apply our experience. Even numbers can be interpreted as classes. Thus, the concept of 'two' can be defined as the class of all couples.

Today it is common to explain aspects of classification in terms of Set Theory. Some of its concepts and notation are sketched here, as they will be found useful in different parts of the book. Although in certain developments of Set Theory a distinction is made between a 'set' and a 'class', they are commonly used interchangeably so that set and class are regarded as equivalent and a sub-set equals a sub-class or species. Set theory is the study of the relations of sets to each other and to their sub-sets. Venn diagrams are commonly used to denote sets and relations between sets. Thus in the Venn diagram in Fig. 2 the outer box could represent the generic need catered for by the firm. This would be known as 'the universal set', and two of its sub-sets (market segments) are shown as circles *A* and *B* within the box. The universal set contains all the elements or species under discussion. Just as it is important to know what we are dividing, so we need to know the appropriate universal set.

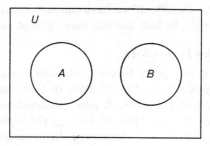

Figure 2

For example, it is easy to sample the wrong population, and so vitiate research results.

Ideally, each segment reflects distinct consumer needs, so that the sub-sets do not overlap to give intersections where consumers are in both segments. In practice it may be impossible to classify the consumers themselves into mutually exclusive sub-sets since some consumers may have multiple needs and thus fall within more than one sub-set.

When two sets intersect to form a sub-set, the properties of the two original sets are combined (e.g. a segment that embraces those customers common to both market *A* and market *B*). The operation can be symbolized as follows:

Symbol	*Used by*	*Term used*
∧ (inverted wedge)	logicians	conjunction
∩ (cap)	mathematicians	intersection
. (dot)	engineers	'and' operation

For example, the intersection of markets A and B to give segment D could be represented by any one of the following:

$$D = A \wedge B, \qquad D = A \cap B, \qquad D = A.B,$$

or diagrammatically as in Fig. 3.

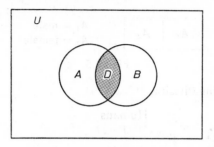

Figure 3

A set D composed of elements of either A or B or both can be represented symbolically by any of the following or as in Fig. 4:

$$D = A \vee B, \qquad D = A \cup B, \qquad D = A+B.$$

Symbol	Used by	Term used
$\vee$ (wedge)	logicians	disjunction
$\cup$ (cup)	mathematicians	union
$+$	engineers	'or' operation

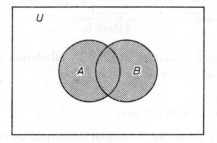

Figure 4

Set D could represent candidates who were either graduates (set A) or members of some professional society (set B), or both.

The universal set can be partitioned (as in the process of division) into exhaustive and mutually exclusive categories. Thus the following

29

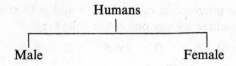

division could be shown as in Fig. 5,

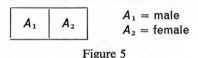

A_1 = male
A_2 = female

Figure 5

and the following division

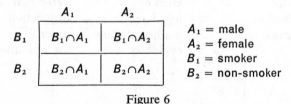

could be shown as a *crossbreak* as in Fig. 6:[1]

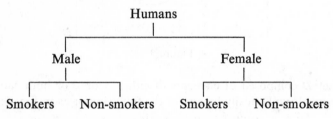

A_1 = male
A_2 = female
B_1 = smoker
B_2 = non-smoker

Figure 6

Crossbreaks are a fundamental form of tabulation used in experimental design, as will be made clear later.

DEFINITION OF TERMS OR SETS

Classification is not possible without definition, as definition determines what is to be included within a class. Of course the main purpose served by definition is to indicate the meaning of a word. The meaning may simply be stipulated for the purpose at hand, or it may be a 'dictionary' definition that indicates the meaning of a

[1] See F. N. Kerlinger, *Foundations of Behavioral Research*, Holt, Rinehart & Winston, New York, 1964.

word to some specific group. The stipulated definition is examined for its utility while the lexical definition is examined for its truth as a factual statement of the way the term is used by some group of people. Whether a definition is stipulated or lexical in purpose, it can take a number of forms. The most appropriate form will depend on purpose. Of course, the same word may have a number of different meanings, and thus different definitions in different contexts. Even a word like 'romantic' can mean twenty-seven different things, some of them contradictory.

Analytic Definitions

The traditional definition is the analytic definition, which states the difference between what we define and the other species within the class to which it belongs. It is essentially a statement of the term's inner attributes or 'connotation'. Hence a definition of economics which has 'the study of the distribution of scarce means among competing ends' makes an important assertion about the nature of economics as a science. An analytic definition of some general class constitutes the concept of that class. Thus 'interpretation' may be defined as a conclusion reached by drawing on experience which does not form explicit evidence for the conclusion. 'Conclusion' is the genus or class to which interpretation belongs. 'Interpretation' is distinguished from other sub-classes of conclusion by the differentia 'reached by drawing on experience that does not form explicit evidence for the conclusion'.

Ideally a definition should be reversible so that 'all conclusions reached by drawing on experience which does not form explicit evidence for the conclusion *are* interpretations'. This symmetrical relationship, though desirable, is difficult to achieve.

The analytic definition has a number of limitations, but it is useful for defining objects that need to be classified for such purposes as counting. For the determination of essential attributes is often a matter of dispute and depends on extra-logical considerations. Thus Cohen and Nagel point out:

Quarrels over the "right" definition are attempts to locate fundamental features. For from a definition is deduced certain consequences. Unless the definition is accepted the consequences will not be. The age-long dispute about the nature of law involves this problem. Is "law" to be construed as a command, as a

31

principle certified by reason or as an agreement? The controversy is not simply about words. It is concerned with making one rather than another aspect of law central so the appropriate consequences may be drawn from it.[1]

Disputes over definition then may be justified when different consequences stem from contrasting definitions. Thus the classical view of authority as 'the institutionalized right to make decisions and to give orders to subordinates on behalf of the company' differs from the view that authority 'is the ability to have one's orders unquestioningly obeyed'. The first definition focuses on legal rights. The second views authority as stemming from the recipient of orders, not from the orders giver, and suggests that it need not be exercised just downwards nor coincide with the allocation of authority indicated in managerial position guides.

We might argue that both definitions have their usefulness for different purposes, and might distinguish them by referring to the first as 'formal authority' and to the second as 'real authority'.

Some disputes over definitions arise, not because different definitions result in varying consequences, but because they concentrate on different ways of measurement, though these may be highly correlated. For example, in their latent structure analysis Campbell and Lazarsfeld regard opinions as merely the observable or manifest counterparts of attitude. The nature of attitude is to be inferred by fitting to the observable (manifest) data an hypothesized model of its latent structure. But Osgood, on the other hand, views opinions as expressions of factual beliefs, and attitudes as expressions of taste. Both views result in different measures, though these may be highly correlated.

Vague Terms

Certain general terms are vague concerning the sub-classes they embrace as they merge with other terms along some continuum. This often stems from the difficulty of determining what combination of conditions is necessary and sufficient for the application of the term. For example, the term 'worker participation' is often defined as 'the shop floor personnel having a say in decisions that affect them ("power with" rather than "power over") or at least having

[1] M. Cohen and E. Nagel, *An Introduction to Logic and Scientific Method*, Harcourt Brace, New York, 1934, p. 230.

the opportunity to influence these decisions'. In practice there are many borderline cases where it is difficult to say whether the occasion is one of participation or of mere consultation. Where one term shades into another along some continuum, and definition is important, its boundaries are determined by the purpose to be served.

There may even be vagueness as to what constitutes the ideal use of the term. Vagueness in terms is perhaps inevitable when a subject or science is young. Rigid definitions can be detrimental to progress, as a subject may not have progressed sufficiently for terms to be analytic in form. The analytic definition, which assumes that essential qualities are known, does not, strictly speaking, admit provisional definition. Yet, in practice, differentia often become superficial when science has progressed. Definitions are hence often regarded as provisional, and likely to be modified or completely changed with the progress of knowledge. There are also no differentia for terms that denote qualities. Thus, blue is a sub-class of colour but what are its differentia?

It has been argued that different definitions of subjects give rise to different frames of reference. But this is similar to the point made earlier by Cohen and Nagel:

'Defining an organization in terms of people co-operating to achieve some goal provides a different frame of reference from one that defines an organization in terms of people being induced through bargaining to contribute to certain goals.'[1]

Analytic definitions were the traditional way of defining as they facilitated classification by seemingly eliminating ambiguity. Their role today is much more modest and the type of definition selected varies with the purpose. However, where an analytic definition is appropriate, then the rules for such a definition are as follows:

1. The denotation of the definition should be the same as the term defined; in other words, a definition should be reversible (a point already made). Thus, defining 'management' as equivalent to 'decision-making' violates this rule.
2. A definition should not be couched in figurative language, as this adds to vagueness and obscures class limits. Thus the definition

[1] Sherman Krupp, *Pattern in Organization Analysis: A Critical Examination*, Holt, Rinehart & Winston, New York, 1961.

of 'organization' as 'the fabric which welds people together' is much too vague. Many definitions in social science fail to illuminate but only confuse.

3. A definition should not be tautologous. Thus to define 'marketing' as 'the process of providing marketing services' may be true, but it is hardly enlightening. (This is not to deny that tautologies can be useful.)

4. A definition should not be negative unless the whole meaning of a term is negative. Thus, it is not helpful to define 'staff' as 'non-operational personnel', since this raises the problem of 'What are operational personnel?'

Synonymous, Contextual, Denotative and Ostensive Definitions

A number of other forms of definition are now common. A synonymous definition may be all that is required. MD may stand for managing director, and 'co-ownership' and 'co-partnership' may be defined as the same. Also, the definition of a word may not be explicitly stated, but may be implicit in some context; thus a contextual definition shows the meaning of a word by its use. For example, if A and B are interdependent and A can predict B's behaviour but B regards A's behaviour as uncertain, then A has power over B. We might even define a word by listing all those to whom it refers. Such a denotative definition of (say) the board of directors would simply list the names of all those who serve on the board. If instead of listing the board members we pointed them out, we would have an ostensive definition of the Board.

Such definitions as the above indicate current practice. Definitions are tending to be assessed more against criteria of utility and usage than against whether the definition reveals true essences. The utility of a definition is related to purpose, which may be simply to reduce vagueness or ambiguity in the use of a term, or to provide some connotative meaning for a term whose denotation is clear.

Definition by Synthesis

For some purposes definition may take the form of showing how the thing to be defined relates to the other elements of the system of which it is part. Thus, the managing director may be defined as the person who is immediately subordinate to the board but who gives direction to all executive officers in the company. This is known as definition by synthesis.

Operational Definitions

A useful definition is the operational definition associated with the philosopher Dewey and the physicist Bridgman, and popularized in psychology by Stevens. Again, the aim is not to give 'true' definitions, but to distinguish objectively between the terms used in theorizing by relating concepts to experience. However, some operational definitions do seem to define the essential nature of a term, and in this way can resemble the analytic definition. For instance, many substances in chemistry are defined in terms of what properties, structure, etc., will be found as consequences following some experimental manipulation of the substance.

An operational definition lists the operations to be carried out and the observations to be made, the performance of which will illuminate the concept to be defined. If the definition shows how to measure some construct, it is known as a measured operational definition. However, an experimental operational definition is conveyed by the experimental details describing what the experimenter did. In this case, operational definitions and contextual definitions resemble each other. Measured operational definitions can be confusing when the same name is given to radically different measures; for example, the different measures of attitude, advertising-page exposure and brand loyalty make it misleading to use these terms without describing their operational measure. Controversy between social scientists and advertising executives over the ease with which attitudes can be changed often results from their each having different operational measures of attitude.

Operational definitions attempt to get agreement by using criteria based on observation, the aim being to experience the concept rather than merely to label it. Here, definition evolves from the common experiences shared by writer and reader. The idea is to illustrate a concept in sufficient detail to convey usage. The aim is to define terms in such a way that they relate to public experience; definitions in terms of private experience do not allow people to communicate effectively. Of course, one of the difficulties in getting out operational definitions is discovering common experiences that can be used as a basis.

Research in the social sciences that appears trivial may in fact be simply an attempt to establish operational measures for certain constructs. Thus, to say 'a job that is a challenge to do gives a person

35

a sense of achievement when completed, and so there will be high output on the job' does not seem very profound. However, to translate this statement into operational terms and situations is of high practical value.

Operational definition is as important in business as it has become in science, where the meaning of a concept depends on the actual scientific procedures used to measure it. When we define, for instance, an 'excellent grade' dictaphone typist as one who produces x lines of type per day, we are using an operational-type definition. There is no debate here about 'essences' of excellent typists, only a specific criterion that allows unambiguous classification. Operational definitions thus reduce the amount of inference required by observers when classifying phenomena.

Operational definitions can be used to define abstract terms. Thus, attitudes are defined operationally in terms of some observable counterpart. These reflect the construct but are not regarded as equivalent to the construct. For example, level of education is not equivalent to a measure of mental sophistication and errors may occur through treating it as such. This problem may be solved by using several available indices rather than by relying on one, though this brings the additional problem of combining the indices into some overall score. This is often done through some statistical procedure. When it is cynically stated that 'intelligence is what intelligence tests measure', the statement emphasizes the necessity of operational definition if the concept is to have practical utility.

Unfortunately, the same statistical measure can represent many different forms of the construct. For example, identical attitude scores may reflect different attitudinal patterns, since identical *average* scores can arise from marking off radically different statements that are alleged to reflect the attitude under consideration.

Operational definitions also have their limitations. All categories cannot be defined in terms of operations and observations. Industrial engineers have still not defined standard performance operationally to ensure that each engineer's concept of this is recognizable and unambiguous.

However detailed the descriptions of operations to be performed, some ambiguity remains. Each method embraced by an operation description covers a group of possible methods, as any operation comprises all operations not specifically excluded by the description. If there is always inherent ambiguity in an operational description, then there will always be difficulty in stating when two operations are to be regarded as the same for the purpose at hand. Ackoff argues that a way of solving this problem is to define in terms of a standard procedure (or standard set of operations) to be carried out under ideal ('best conceivable') laid-down circumstances, and to allow for deviations from this in the results obtained.[1] Getting out a standard procedure for ideal conditions is not easy, while techniques for measuring the actual deviations from the ideal may on occasions raise greater problems than they solve. (Industrial engineers will recognize Mundel's objective rating as being an attempt at this type of operational definition.) Ackoff acknowledges such difficulties but rightly regards his recommendation as an ideal to be pursued.

What type of definition is the most appropriate depends purely on purpose. An ostensive definition (e.g. 'such a man as Churchill') can often be supplied where there is likely to be doubt. A real problem is to maintain consistency of definition to avoid confusion.

Although, as pointed out, there may be valid reasons for disputes over definition, it is also true that some questions, put forward as serious questions about real events, are in reality merely questions about what something should be called. Thus there are arguments about whether the company is market-oriented or production-oriented, whether management is centralized or decentralized, etc., instead of concentrating on descriptions of actual practices and the consequences that arise from such practices.

LANGUAGE, SIGNS AND SYMBOLS

Descriptive statements, definitions and classifications are expressed in words, the choice of which is important. A language is simply a set of symbols that stand for the ideas and objects we perceive. Language and perception form an interacting system with language helping to mould perception and perceptions influencing language, since sensations are labelled, classified and interrelated by the use of language and concepts based on language. What we perceive may be distorted to fit a mode of expression or language pattern, and narrowness in language may lead to narrowness in perception.

The language selected may conjure up false analogies in the mind of the reader. Thus, industrial sociological literature speaks of

[1] Russell L. Ackoff, *Scientific Method*, John Wiley & Sons Inc., New York, 1962, ch. 5.

'democratic' versus 'autocratic' leadership styles. Such terms are emotive and give rise to an immediate bias. Yet they are not factually descriptive since so-called democratic leaders in industry are not necessarily elected, while, on the other hand, leaders in democratic government govern by the consent but not necessarily according to the will of the people.

Susanne Langer distinguishes sign from symbol. The object constituting a sign is present when the sign is perceived, whereas a symbol merely brings to mind the thing being symbolized.[1] Lasswell *et al.*, more explicitly, regard signs as the physical devices (e.g. the printed word) that disseminate meaning, while symbols themselves possess meaning.[2] It is argued that the use of symbols is the distinguishing feature of man enabling him to think abstractly.

There may only be a very remote connection between the object itself and what it symbolizes. Thus, Hayakawa makes the following observation:

> 'Hence a sun-blackened skin, once considered ugly because it symbolized work, is now considered beautiful because it symbolizes leisure . . .
>
> 'People from outside the South often find it difficult to understand how many white Southerners accept close physical contact with Negro servants and yet become extremely upset at the idea of sitting beside Negroes in restaurants or buses. The attitude of the Southerner rests on the fact that the ministrations of a Negro servant—even personal care, such as nursing—have the symbolic implication of social inequality; while admission of Negroes to buses, restaurants, and nonsegregated schools has the symbolic implication of social equality.'[3]

Consequently, the same object may symbolize different things to different people depending on their experience and value system. This is one of the difficulties encountered in establishing invariable relationships between stimulus and response in human behaviour. People react not so much to the object itself as to what it symbolizes,

---

[1] Osgood, the psychologist, uses the words 'significate' for the sense in which sign is used here and 'sign' for the way symbol is defined.
[2] H. D. Lasswell, *Language of Politics*, M.I.T. Press, Cambridge, Mass., 1968, p. 21.
[3] S. I. Hayakawa, *Language in Thought and Action*, Harcourt Brace, New York and George Allen & Unwin, London, p. 25.

that is, to how they perceive it. This differs from one person to another, as does their reaction to it. People at different levels in the management hierarchy tend to have diverse perceptions arising from their different experiences. Such differing viewpoints are inevitable; identically expressed viewpoints on all topics are grounds for suspecting totalitarianism. However, a lack of understanding that varied viewpoints can be honestly held may lead managers and workers into behaving in a manner that seems to deny to each the validity of the other's position. But some honestly held viewpoints can still be unjust. Thus Bertrand Russell comments:

> 'The only way in which a society can live for any length of time without violent strife is by establishing social justice, and social justice appears to each man to be injustice if he is persuaded that he is superior to his neighbours.'[1]

Emotive Language

It has already been pointed out that classification can reflect an attitude as well as a purpose. The same applies to the choice of words. We might recall Bertrand Russell's 'I am firm, you are obstinate, he is pig-headed'. Evaluative terms like 'disloyal' are not factually descriptive terms but reflect attitudes. So often in a report the reader only goes to the first paragraph to discover the writer's attitudes and bias. This is not to condemn emotive language (as there may be occasions when we must reveal our feelings), but is simply a reminder that any communication carries not only a message but also a tone.

There is a danger of reification in naming where an abstraction is classified as a real thing. A name does not prove the existence of the thing named. Phrases like 'union mentality' may be used as convenient descriptions of behaviour. However, it is also important to remember that such collectives are fictitious and it may be less misleading to speak of 'the way the people who run the union think'. A most common form of reification is the firm itself—'The firm must be put above all else', as if it had some end over and above the aims of the various power groups that determine its direction. Reification is also indulged in to give the impression that decisions are being dictated by forces beyond the power of the decision-maker, e.g.

[1] Bertrand Russell, *The Art of Philosophizing and Other Essays*, Philosophical Library, New York, 1968, p. 4.

'Policy dictated that we declare redundancy', or 'Luck went against us, and that's all there is to it'.

It is also easy to change a symbol and to believe that reality in some way has also changed. Thus a sales director may be called a 'marketing director', the company believing that it is now up to date and market-orientated though nothing else has changed. It is common to give people elaborate titles to avoid conflict. Thus a man who is redundant may be called 'group co-ordinator' in the hope that the title disguises reality.

MEANING OF STATEMENTS AND EXPRESSIONS

In one sense the context in which a term is used always affects its meaning, regardless of the type of definition adopted. Thus Clarence Irving Lewis argues that statements are combinations of terms, but the syntax of the statement itself affects the meaning of the terms.[1] Therefore the meaning of a term (excepting such words as 'the') cannot be entirely divorced from its context.

The interpretation of the meaning of a statement or expression is important, as we cannot talk about the truth or falsity of statements till we have established their meaning. Lewis rightly argues that statements must be considered as a whole in order to gauge their meaning, and that that meaning will be something more than the sum of the meanings of the individual terms.

There are many viewpoints about the meaning of statements or expressions. As in the definition of terms, these various viewpoints tend to stress either denotative or connotative aspects. Some emphasize denotation. Thus there is the popular view that the meaning of a statement is the object to which the statement refers. On this basis, the statement 'hourly paid workers employed by the company' would be equivalent to 'shop-floor personnel employed by the company', or to 'union members employed by the company', if each had the same referent; but there is a difference in emphasis which alters their meaning.

A more sophisticated denotation approach is that taken by linguistic philosophy. Here the meaning of an expression is its use; so discovering meaning depends on finding the occasions when a statement is being correctly used. Unfortunately this ignores the

[1] C. I. Lewis, *Analysis of Knowledge and Valuation*, La Salle, Illinois, Open Court, 1946.

fact that the connotation of an expression must often be known before it can be correctly applied. Thus Gellner in a severe criticism of linguistic philosophy makes this point:

> 'The meaning of the term "of one's own free will" is not defined in terms of smiling bridegrooms, but on the contrary the behaviour of smiling bridegrooms is interpreted in such a way as to make those terms applicable. The interpretation may be mistaken.'[1]

Analysis of the denotation of an expression may reveal that it is being used to denote two different references in the same context. These uses may not always be obvious. Consequently, commenting on the so-called management principle that 'specialists should have no authority, but should only advise', one sociologist points out that by another management principle, 'authority should be commensurate with responsibility', specialists, having no authority, should also have no responsibility. This is a fallacy of equivocation, since the original use of the term 'authority' referred to 'authority over staff in other departments', and did not include authority over the specialist's own subordinates, nor suggest that a specialist should have no authority, for instance, to authorize money payments.

The denotation of an expression may be ambiguous. An expression or word is ambiguous if it has two entirely different meanings; it is vague if there is doubt about its limits or if the concept varies in degree.

Vagueness often arises when references to one state merge into another along a scale; the reader will recall the example of the difficulty of separating participation and consultation. This is not to deny the utility, and at times the necessity, of labelling different parts of some continuum without committing oneself to the viewpoint that each category is discrete; the argument that borderline cases are difficult to distinguish does not imply that the categories cannot in general be demarcated.

Operational definitions are the best way to achieve some precision and avoid vagueness—preferably using the operational definitions from research work concerned with establishing or manipulating the concepts. However, this may be dangerous if the operational

---

[1] Ernest Gellner, *Words and Things*, Pelican Books, Harmondsworth, 1968, p. 37. In spite of Gellner's criticism the utility of the approach is well demonstrated in *Thinking With Concepts* by John Wilson (Cambridge University Press, London, 1963).

definitions suggest extremes. For example, classifying people into 'prejudiced' and 'not-prejudiced', or companies into 'centralized' and 'de-centralized', can be misleading, as it involves a two-valued orientation. It is a favourite argument to present a dichotomy of alternatives to force an audience to take sides. 'In this labour dispute we must either stick to our guns, or go under.' 'We must either work as one, or have anarchy.' The presentation of such arguments is often compelling, as they appear to stem from wisdom rather than from an inability to see that a middle course is possible.

There are viewpoints that emphasize the connotative aspects of meaning. Charles Morris argues that the meaning of any sign (including words) is its effect on the subject perceiving it, namely, his disposition to behave in a certain way to some particular object.

Similarly, other approaches emphasize behavioural response. Here the meaning of a term will depend on the experience associated with it. As a consequence, since no two people have the same background of experience, no term or statement has the same precise connotative meaning for any two people though they may agree on denotation. Thus, to say that two people respond differently to the same thing is a loose way of speaking, since the object has not the same symbolic reference for different people. Of course, the overlap in connotation of words among people within the same culture is apt to be large; but market researchers who give to prospective buyers a concept statement on a proposed new product, are often surprised to find how the interpretations of the words in the statement vary.

Osgood, the psychologist, subscribes to a connotative view. He argues that meaning is an intervening variable that operates between situation and behaviour; it results from receiving stimuli and is a necessary antecedent to behaviour. He distinguishes between meaning and attitude, arguing that attitude is only one dimension of meaning and, as currently measured, seldom provides sufficient information for prediction. He puts forwards the semantic differential to measure the meaning of any concept for an individual. In the semantic differential the concept or object (e.g. brand or product whose meaning is being determined) is evaluated on a seven-point scale for each of a series of bipolar attributes, e.g. strong–weak. Factor analysis has led to the identification of three distinct factors. (Factor analysis is a statistical technique for determining whether the variance in an original set of variables or factors can be accounted for by a smaller number of basic categories or factors. It is also a way of defining one construct in terms of other constructs, e.g. to establish the relationship [if any] between, say, guilt, shame, anxiety, vigilance and fear.)

1. Evaluation: Good—bad
   (extent to which object judged favourable or unfavourable).
2. Potency: Strong—weak
   (amount of strength needed to deal with object).
3. Activity: Fast—slow
   (how quick activity should be in relation to object).

Osgood points out that the essence of the technique lies in selecting a sample of descriptive polar terms. This sample should be representative of the ways in which meaningful judgments can vary, yet not be so large that it is unwieldy in practice. Osgood's definition of meaning is less inclusive than Morris's since, though it emphasizes the subject's disposition to react in a certain way because of some sign, it excludes the specification of the object towards which he is prepared to behave in the way described.

MEANINGFULNESS OF STATEMENTS AND EXPRESSIONS

A statement can have meaning but it may not be 'meaningful' in the sense that it may not be significant or useful in solving some particular problem. Two views of meaningfulness can be distinguished, associated with logical positivism and pragmatism respectively.

Logical Positivism

The logical positivists distinguish between analytic and synthetic statements. The truth of an analytic statement follows from the definitions of words occurring in it, as in mathematics. But the truth of synthetic statements cannot be established merely by reference to the syntactic and semantic rules of language; it must be established empirically. There is no difficulty in distinguishing analytic statements, as they are deductions from definitions. The question is to test synthetic statements for their significance. The positivists developed a test known as the 'verifiability criterion'. A sentence that did not conform to the verifiability criterion was either analytic (hence needing no confirming) or nonsensical. Another way of showing their position is

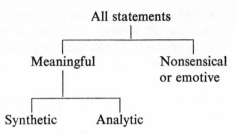

A statement is only meaningful if it either says something which can be verified or follows as a deduction from the meaning of the words it contains. If there are no observations relevant to the truth or falsehood of a non-analytic proposition, the statement is nonsensical or meaningless. Thus A. J. Ayer has observed:

> 'We say that a sentence is factually significant to any given person, if, and only if, he knows how to verify the proposition which it purports to express—that is, if he knows what observations would lead him, under certain conditions, to accept the proposition as being true, or reject it as being false . . .
>
> 'A simple and familiar example of such a proposition is the proposition that there are mountains on the farther side of the moon. No rocket has yet been invented which would enable me to go and look at the farther side of the moon, so that I am unable to decide the matter by actual observation. But I do know what observations would decide it for me, if, as is theoretically conceivable, I were once in a position to make them. And therefore I say that the proposition is verifiable in principle, if not in practice, and is accordingly significant . . .
>
> 'But until he makes us understand how the proposition that he wishes to express would be verified, he fails to communicate anything to us.'[1]

There is a relationship between analytic propositions and *a priori* statements. An *a priori* statement is one whose truth or falsity is established independently of observation. Hence analytic propositions are *a priori* since they stem from the rules of language.

There is also a relationship between *a posteriori* statements (whose truth or falsity is established by reference to empirical fact) and synthetic propositions. Understanding the meaning of some *a posteriori* statement (e.g. 'the market share has dropped') does

[1] A. J. Ayer, *Language, Truth and Logic*, Gollancz, London, 1964, pp. 35–6.

not in itself give any guidance to its truth, which depends on empirical fact. Perhaps all synthetic statements are *a posteriori*, though some philosophers (e.g. Arthur Pap) have argued for the existence of *a priori* synthetic statements whose truth or falsity can be established independently of observation but which are not simply deductions from the rules of language, e.g. the proposition that 'something's happened'.

The logical positivist's verifiability criterion acts as a check on establishing *a priori* generalizations, and also denies the existence of *a priori* synthetic knowledge. Although the principle of verifiability refers to statements, it might also be applied to terms. It may be argued that operational definitions provide for the verifiability of terms as they relate to shared experiences.

A proposition may not be falsified because it is worded in a vague and ambiguous form. Thus one well-known writer in marketing refers to, 'The belief that within the limits imposed on the persuader, a purchaser will not buy against his own perceived interest.' If this is meant to be a synthetic proposition and not just a tautology, it must be restated in more operational terms—and this the writer does not do.

Logical positivism, as associated with A. J. Ayer, Moritz Schlick and Rudolph Carnap, 'rules out from the realm of meaningful discourse' ethical, aesthetic, religious and value statements. The dismissal of value and ethical judgments as merely emotive statements has led Blanshard to speak of logical positivism leading to a 'Boo-Hurrah' theory of ethics. This in turn means 'no-one can make a mistake on a moral issue, nor correct mistaken ideas on morals, so that the very concept of justice has no meaning'. Blanshard's view may appear extreme. Because the truth of some ethical principle cannot be established, it does not follow that the practical utility of some ethical principle cannot be established. Eminent philosophers like Popper have argued that some non-analytic statements may be significant although they cannot be falsified. But, to insist that all theories in the final analysis be *directly* testable would unduly limit the methods of verification. Philosophers such as Quine and White argue that no sharp distinction can be drawn between analytic and synthetic statements. The principle of verifiability itself appears neither clearly analytic nor synthetic, but it has never been labelled emotive or nonsensical by logical positivists. Sometimes the context does not make it clear whether a statement is meant to be taken as empirical fact or merely as a deduction from a definition or classification.

The significance of many statements or terms depends on their contextual setting. Until this is known one cannot consider whether the statement is true or false.

The principle of verifiability may be an attempt to distinguish those hypotheses which can be tested by observation from those that can not. It is a criterion for distinguishing hypotheses before investing time and energy in trying to verify the nonsensical. It is a reminder that a problem should be worded in such a way as to suggest how it might be tested empirically; this can be difficult, as the connection between complex problems and observable data is often remote. It is also an attempt to classify different types of knowledge. People put forward statements that they believe are synthetic when they are not, e.g. 'The problem is to get the right marketing mix and then we will achieve an optimum allocation of resources.' Such statements lead an audience to ask for proof when they are merely an extension of a definition.

It is pointless to try to resolve some non-empirical problem by empirical means. Thus, although we can legitimately ask what led to a fall-off in sales, to ask whether the fall-off was inevitable is merely to speculate about what might have happened or might have been done. A problem must be framed in operational terms if it is to be resolvable empirically. Thus, 'Is advertising doing a good job?' requires restatement in terms more operational.

Pragmatism

The doctrine of pragmatism (or, as developed by Dewey, 'instrumentalism') developed in the USA at the end of the last century and is associated with William James, Charles Saunders Peirce and John Dewey. In pragmatism, human ideas when translated into action are viewed as responses to problems, and their significance depends on the extent to which the action is instrumental in solving the problem. Thus, a pragmatist might argue that even the ethical statement 'x is good' should be turned into a verifiable hypothesis, e.g. 'x is good for purpose y given condition z'. It asks whether it makes any difference whether a statement is true. The meaningfulness of a statement on this basis depends on its consequences if it were true. Only statements which have practical consequences can be significant: a statement is of no significance if its truth or falsity makes no difference to decision. The 'cash value' (or meaningfulness) of a statement or even of a theory, can be assessed in terms of the possible difference it would make to a decision if it were true or false. Pragmatism is an underlying philosophy in many business decisions. It is even reflected in a current view of information. McKay points out that to gain information is to have a change in expectations (i.e. disposition to respond) caused by the data; data that does not do so adds nothing new. ('For the Archbishop of Canterbury to declare he believes in God is hardly information but to say he doesn't is.')

Interpretations of pragmatism varied among its adherents. To Peirce, practical consequences referred to those consequences which could be inspected and investigated. In this sense Peirce's criterion for significance is similar to the principle of verification. (In fact, both the verification principle and pragmatism aim at clarifying meaning in terms of showing significance and possible truth.) For James, practical consequences referred to consequences capable of affecting behaviour. Thus, only Peirce's interpretation offered an objective criterion for establishing the significance of statements.

Chapter 3

THE DEDUCTIVE PATTERN OF EXPLANATION

ROLE OF EXPLANATION IN PROBLEM-SOLVING

An analysis of a problematic situation that includes an explanation of its origins helps to turn a perceived difficulty into a specific problem and offers guidance in deciding appropriate action. Also, if we hope to prevent the repetition of some problem, then it needs to be explained. A reduction in sales that is the result of poor field selling is a different problem from one resulting from competitors offering higher trade discounts. Similarly, an increase in the proportion of 'rejects' because of an arbitrary tightening-up of inspection standards requires different managerial action from a situation resulting from poor machine maintenance.

A problematic situation is merely a stimulus that directs attention; it does not necessarily direct action. The nature of the problem must be stated in a way that arouses ideas about a solution. Scientists and others have wrestled for a long time with problems which they were able to solve rapidly once they were restated. It seems that the restated problem enabled the recall of ideas and concepts not aroused by the original statement. A statement of a problem that includes an explanation about how it arose can help in the formulation of the necessary corrective and preventive action.

1. There is the *deductive* pattern, in which an event is explained by showing how it follows if some assumption, hypothesis, law, theory or model is accepted as true.
2. There is the *statistical* generalization, where the event to be explained is shown to be probable on the evidence (though such demonstration, in itself, would not necessarily constitute an explanation).
3. There is the *teleological* type of explanation which explains in terms of goals sought or functions performed.
4. Finally, we have the *genetic* type of explanation, which is essentially an historical approach showing how past events have

led up to the existing state of affairs. This draws on the other three approaches.

Meehan offers the following as criteria for judging the 'usefulness' of an explanation:

'Four points are particularly important: first, the *scope* of the explanation, the range of events to which it can be applied; second, explanations differ in *precision*, in the accuracy of the expectations they generate and of the control procedures they imply; third, explanations differ in *power*, and the amount of control over an empirical situation that they permit; finally, explanations differ in *reliability*, in the amount of confidence we place on their use.'[1]

These criteria, though applying more especially to scientific explanation, can be applied to explanation in general.

ASSUMPTIONS AND HYPOTHESES

Assumptions lie behind all reasoning. Often these are taken for granted and people fail to recognize that assumptions have been made. Thus, a manager may assume that people will resist change, or that all human relations problems result from poor communication. Some assumptions are so plausible that they are not likely to be queried except by those with relevant experience. Thus it would appear reasonable to spend on advertising in a test market in proportion to the expenditure planned when sales are national, given that the market test reflects the national launch in miniature. Yet experience shows that the cost per impression is often greater per consumer in a test market than at the national level, as test marketing involves using local advertising media.

Assumptions are even behind the drive to scientific inquiry, for example, assumptions that there is a mathematical order in nature, that evolutionary tendencies are at work, or that all behaviour is (at least in principle) explicable and predictable. At the more mundane level, we all assume as a result of experience that food and water will satisfy hunger and thirst.

A belief may or may not be true. The idea behind science is the testing of belief by the systematic collection of evidence. In

[1] Eugene J. Meehan, *Explanation in Social Science: A System Paradigm*, The Dorsey Press, Homewood, Illinois, 1968, p. 115.

consequence, the roles of faith, authority and intuition as the basis of belief, are diminished.

When a general assumption that relates some set of events is exposed and put forward for testing, it is regarded as an hypothesis and the process of formulating and testing hypotheses is known as 'induction'. An hypothesis is a proposition setting out a relationship between two or more items whose truth or falsity is yet to be determined. A problem asks a question about the relationship between variables or events. An hypothesis merely translates the problem into forms that facilitate testing essentially in terms of establishing relationships between events or variables.

This is not to suggest that all the facts are first assembled to discover a principle that might underlie them. An organizing hypothesis must come before any systematic collection of facts, since this determines relevance. However, as an inquiry begins, hypothesis development and the gathering of further facts are carried out simultaneously. The aim of examining an explanation is to discover the hidden assumptions, and to recognize that such statements are provisional and should be treated as hypotheses that require testing. Of course, an hypothesis is a generalization formulated from experience. It does not materialize from nothing, but results from experience being employed on current events in order to help explain them.

There may be reasons for thinking some hypothesis is true. It might be consistent with what we already believe to be true, and be supported by common sense and intuition. However, subjective certainty does not guarantee the truth of an hypothesis; what seems to be true beyond doubt may be well worth doubting. Yet it may be difficult to question assumptions if they are beliefs that are emotionally held (e.g. 'God will provide'). In fact, people perhaps seldom take assumptions and test them so much as they take beliefs and simply seek evidence to support them.

Testing Hypotheses

The probability of an hypothesis being true is established by taking a sample of its logical consequences and confirming that these are true. There is a need of such validating evidence; yet, unless an hypothesis seems probable on other grounds, confirming consequences may still appear inadequate. These 'other grounds' are concerned with how the hypothesis fits into our existing set of beliefs.

If it is consistent and reinforces current beliefs, then the hypothesis is more readily believed. Where an hypothesis does not cohere or, at least, is not congruent with existing knowledge, the confirmation of predicted consequences is less convincing. There is a great deal of evidence for extra-sensory perception, but it may still be rejected on the grounds that it 'just does not make sense'. On the other hand there is not much validating evidence for psychotherapy, but it may be accepted because its explanations form a self-consistent, unified whole.[1]

Lewis argues that an empirical belief can be rationally justified if it can be shown to be congruent with existing empirically established beliefs. Blanshard regards coherence as the criterion of truth. These two positions differ. If two beliefs cohere, then one logically entails the other, but if beliefs are congruent, the truth of one merely increases the probability of the truth of the other where truth is established through empirical inquiry.

We may have difficulty in getting an hypothesis rejected if others insist on creating new and 'unlikely' hypotheses to explain away findings unfavourable to the hypothesis. Take the hypothesis 'advertising has affected sales'. To counter the argument that sales have not increased, the qualification made is that advertising prevented a decrease. The qualification that this is not the way advertising works is put forward to counter the argument that consumer attitudes towards the product have not changed. The argument that sales have been just as good where there has been no advertising is countered by the argument that past advertising is now having an effect in these areas.

The conditions for the formulation of an hypothesis are that it should explain and be formulated so that consequences can be deduced which are verifiable. Ideally these consequences should be 'surprising', as there is always a danger of creating an hypothesis to explain events and then 'confirming' the hypothesis by showing that these events are the logical consequences of the hypothesis. One suspects that this circular reasoning is common in social science. There is never any difficulty in devising some hypothesis to explain what is already known. The problem is to devise an hypothesis that explains the present facts but also leads to the prediction and confirmation of what is currently thought unlikely to be true.

[1] See Joseph F. Rychlak, *A Philosophy of Science for Personality Theory*, Houghton Mifflin Co., Boston, Mass., 1968.

In testing an hypothesis, we construct a hypothetical proposition defined symbolically as:

If *A* is *B*   then   *C* is *D*

antecedent   consequent

where the assumption (or hypothesis) is the antecedent and the likely result(s) of the assumption is the consequent, e.g.

If workers always resist   they will resent the proposal
change that affects them   then   to give them a share in company profits.

antecedent   consequent

However, where the antecedent does not include the consequent simply as a matter of strict logic, the alleged consequence may not in fact necessarily follow. In such circumstances, showing the consequence to be untrue would not disprove the hypothesis.

Where the consequent is a matter of logical entailment and can be shown to be untrue in fact, then the universal assumption about workers always resisting change can be rejected. Where the consequent appears to be true in fact, this raises the probability that the assumption is also true. An hypothesis must be consistent with the available evidence, while its opposite must be in conflict with that evidence (or the evidence would be consistent both with an hypothesis and its opposite!).

Where appropriate, an hypothesis may sometimes be tested more directly by being split into antecedent and consequent, e.g.

If people are workers   then   they will always resist change that affects them.

antecedent   consequent

Where both antecedent and consequent are continuous variables, the relationship between the two may be one of correlation, with the antecedent the independent variable and the consequent the dependent variable, e.g. the relationship between prices and amount sold.

If the proposition 'if *A* then *C*' were true, then affirming the antecedent or denying the consequent would give a conclusion that is certain. Symbolically, affirming the antecedent could be shown by any of the following:

(1) If A then C: (2) If A is B then C is D:
    A, A is B,
    $\therefore$ C. $\therefore$ C is D.

(or where p and q stand for antecedent and consequent respectively and the symbol $\Rightarrow$ replaces 'if . . . then')

(3) $p \Rightarrow q$:
    p,
    $\therefore$ q.

Denying the consequent could be shown as:

(1) If A then C: (2) If A is B then C is D:
    not C, C is not D,
    $\therefore$ not A. $\therefore$ A is not B.
(3) $p \Rightarrow q$:
    $\sim q$ (not-q),
    $\therefore$ $\sim p$ (not-p).

We speak of the validity of arguments and the truth of premises and conclusions. Thus we may have a valid argument even if premises and conclusions are false, e.g. 'If the workers are happy, then the company is prosperous. This company is not prosperous. Therefore the workers are not happy.' The conclusion may be false, but the inference is valid. Similarly, a conclusion may be true even if the argument is invalid.

Every hypothesis contains some consequences. These consequences stem from the definitions of the words used in the hypothesis. If the hypothesis is true, so must the consequence be true. But an hypothesis itself is tested by confirming that the consequences are true in fact. If we could verify every consequence we could verify the hypothesis, but this is seldom possible. Hence, according to Popper we must emphasize falsification rather than verification.[1] Thus Turner comments:[2]

'Let us say the term "depression" contains in its definition the predicates "national income below such and such level", "rate of

[1] K. R. Popper, *The Logic of Scientific Discovery*, Hutchinson, London, 1954.
[2] M. B. Turner, *Philosophy and the Science of Behaviour*, Appleton-Century-Crofts Inc., New York, 1967, p. 147.

unemployment above such and such level," etc. Proceeding to test by falsification we hold true the hypothesis, depression, so long as each test of a possible predicate results in the verdict "true". Thus we hold the hypothesis provisionally true until it is falsified . . .

'In the present example, our definition (of the country being in "a state of depression") contains a finite set of predicates. Therefore, our hypothesis is in principle both verifiable and falsifiable. Ultimately, one strategy of testing is as good as another. But what is the case when the statement, or hypothesis, has an unlimited number of predicates? What if the hypothesis is a scientific law? Then under the conditions of testability, the hypothesis is falsifiable but not verifiable. Because of this fact, Karl Popper has proposed analysing the logic and method of science under conventions that are deductivist rather than inductivist, and that stress falsification rather than verification.'

In Popper's view the hypothesis comes first and is accepted until falsified. He calls his approach deductivism in contrast to induction where universal hypotheses are visualized as being developed from the particulars of experience. In deductivism a statement is meaningful not because it is in principle verifiable but because it is falsifiable, as a general statement can be falsified but not conclusively verified; confirming the consequence of an hypothesis is a necessary but never a sufficient condition for the establishment of the truth of the antecedent. On the other hand, it could be argued that non-universal hypotheses (e.g. 'some people are aggressive when frustrated') can be verified but never completely falsified as, unlike universal statements, all tests of scientific statements are subject to sampling error. This is recognized by statisticians in the way they formulate their results.

The problem of what constitutes an adequate test of an hypothesis is not straightforward. Thus, Churchman points out:[1] 'Hypothesis- and theory-testing are delicate operations, and, as yet, in the history of science we have no very clear ideas how they should be performed.' It is common to apply a double standard in judging evidence; one standard for evidence that supports one's case, and another standard to evidence that does not. Thus, survey

[1] W. Churchman, *Prediction and Optimal Decision*, Prentice-Hall Inc., Englewood Cliffs, N.J., 1966, p. 78.

evidence may be quoted to support a position, while similar evidence may be rejected ('people only say that') if the evidence conflicts with their prejudgments.

The mere accumulation of observations that support an hypothesis is not enough since they may all simply be testing but one aspect of the hypothesis. Predicted consequences that do not conform to the facts may not lead to a rejection of the hypothesis immediately. There may be grounds for suspicion that the measurement of the consequences is at fault. For example, we may set up an hypothesis that salesmen have a considerable influence on the amount a buyer buys. We test the hypothesis by asking buyers, but replies do not acknowledge such influence. We may rightly believe that there are reasons why such replies do not represent the true position and the measure itself may be rejected rather than the hypothesis.

In spite of the difficulties in testing hypotheses to ensure reasonable certainty, there is usually much that can be done to test whether the hypothesis is likely. All too often statements are believed to be true or false simply on the grounds that the statement could possibly be true or false. Thus, establishing that a person had the opportunity or motive to sabotage some particular project does not establish the fact that he did so. Furthermore, reasons may be quoted in support of a proposition which are irrelevant to proof. Thus, a person may ask whether a particular test is valid and be faced with the reply that the test has been in use for over ten years. Similarly, negative evidence is not proof. Thus, to argue that there have been no complaints about a product does not prove that the consumer finds it satisfactory. Finally, a proposition is not disproved by quoting the unpleasant consequences if it were true, e.g. 'on your argument we'd be heading for bankruptcy'—when perhaps the company is!

In practice, there are few assumptions that are universally true; they are mainly statements of extreme likelihood. It could easily be demonstrated that 'all work people on all occasions resist change' is not true. On the other hand, to say that some work people on some occasions resist change is hardly informative. Thus, when people speak of 'workers resisting change that affects them', they simply mean that the statement is a statistical generalization. If we find that some workers have not resisted changes that affect them on one occasion, we have not disproved the assertion that workers *generally* resist such change. There is a danger of course in dismissing evidence because it is inconsistent with current beliefs;

55

decisions are too often reached before any objective examination of the evidence.

Polya[1] uses the word 'plausibility' for comparative probability and sets out a number of patterns of plausible inference, e.g.

(1) If A then B
B
$\therefore A$ more credible

(2) If A then B
B credible
$\therefore A$ somewhat credible

(3) If A then B
not A
$\therefore B$ less credible

(4) If A then B
A more credible
$\therefore B$ more credible

The essential point to note is that the conclusions cannot be more credible than is claimed for them in the premises. While confirming the consequent of a statement adds to the probability of its truth, a number of likely consequences need to be tested, since the confirmation of one single consequence is not likely to be crucially significant. We do not conclusively verify an hypothesis as fail to disprove it. A. J. Ayer comments:

'Indeed, it will be our contention that no proposition, other than a tautology, can possibly be anything more than a probable hypothesis. . . .

'A hypothesis cannot be conclusively confuted any more than it can be conclusively verified.'[2]

Rival hypotheses

In testing hypotheses, the problem is that of rival hypotheses. A rival hypothesis is an alternative hypothesis that can equally explain all the relevant facts observed. Rival hypotheses must be made, particularly unwelcome ones, as these are most likely to be ignored. A test that shows one of the rival hypotheses to be untenable is a 'crucial test'. Such tests only eliminate rival hypotheses and do not conclusively show the one remaining to be true. In choosing rival hypotheses, it is not just a matter of the number or combinations or denials of consequence; judgment is needed to assess the significance of the consequence for the truth or falsity of the hypothesis. Also, the two rival hypotheses may not be true, the true one may embrace both of them or they might be equivalent, differing only in their

[1] G. Polya, *Patterns of Plausible Inference*, Princeton University Press, Princeton, N.J., 1954.

[2] A. J. Ayer, *Language, Truth and Logic*, Gollancz, London, 1964, pp. 37–8.

wording or symbolic formulation. In any case it is not always just a matter of choosing between one hypothesis and another, but between alternative sets of hypotheses.

It may not be possible to demonstrate on a factual basis that one set of hypotheses is much more likely than another. In such cases the criterion of simplicity might be useful. Simplicity can be interpreted in a number of ways; one hypothesis can have greater 'simplicity of understanding', in the sense that it has a higher prior probability of being true, because of its consistency with existing knowledge or, better still, because it harmonizes with existing facts and helps to illuminate connections among them. One hypothesis may have greater simplicity in that it is not so complex. Complex hypotheses are often difficult to falsify. Of course hypotheses can appear simple in formulation but require background knowledge to understand them, so that there must be simplicity 'not only in the equations but also in the text'.

The weighing of evidence is a very real problem where rival hypotheses receive support of different kinds. The only approach so far put forward for weighing the *relative value* of different types of evidence is that provided by probability theory, but the extent to which this provides a comprehensive rational methodology is a matter of dispute.

One final point should be re-emphasized. Many problems are formulated in ways that disguise the fact that they consist of an hypothesis to be tested. For example, a company executive might ask, 'Will a price cut lead to retaliatory action on the part of competitors?' The question is better posed as 'To what extent do we have evidence to support the hypothesis that a price cut will lead to retaliatory action by competitors?' The first question seems to elicit merely opinion, the second question demands consideration of evidence.

Commonsense opinion is no substitute for examination of the evidence. The knowledge constituting commonsense is generally vague and, as Randall and Buchler point out, this very lack of precision makes it have high face validity but gives it only a limited capacity to explain.

'... by its nature makes little pretension to exactness; its "risk" of error is less. The purposes of description and communication for which it is designed are adequately satisfied.

'But if commonsense is thus essentially reliable knowledge, it is so at the expense of being narrow, static, and unenlightening, and only in so far as our needs are of a rudimentary character.

'In general, then, there can be no doubt that the most evident distinguishing characteristic between commonsense and empirical science is the far greater degree of abstractness of the latter.'[1]

DEDUCTIVE AND INDUCTIVE ARGUMENT

What may be a legitimate inductive argument may not be valid deductively, since a valid deductive argument requires the premises to imply the conclusion. A deductive system is one in which the truth or falsity of a few propositions determines the truth or falsity of the others. Modern symbolic or mathematical logic deals with deductive argument and goes well beyond the system devised by Aristotle. In the nineteenth century Boole's work on truth functions conceived logic as an algebra, thus allowing deduction by mathematical rules. Peano, and particularly the mathematician Frege, made further significant advances and the subject was systematized by Whitehead and Russell in *Principia Mathematica*. There are now many different additional systems of logic. I will not deal with symbolic logic, as no short exposition could do justice to the subject. But the following advice by Beardsley[2] on arranging an argument can help in avoiding confusion and facilitate understanding.

He first distinguishes convergent, divergent, and serial arguments. In a convergent argument, several different reasons converge to support the one conclusion, e.g.

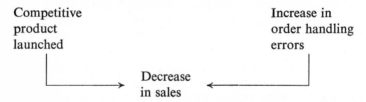

In a divergent argument, the one reason diverges to support more than one conclusion, e.g.

---

[1] J. H. Randall Jr and J. Buchler, *Philosophy: An Introduction*, Barnes & Noble Inc., New York, pp. 65–6.

[2] M. C. Beardsley, *Thinking Straight*, Prentice-Hall Inc., Englewood Cliffs, N.J., 1950, p. 6.

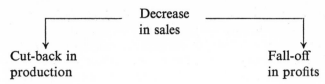

In a serial argument, one conclusion forms the reason for further conclusions, e.g.

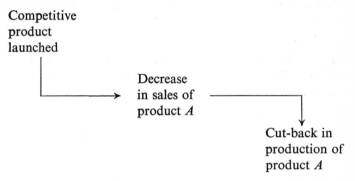

An argument may be a mixture of convergent, divergent and serial arguments.

Beardsley recommends the following procedure for rearranging an argument to expose its structure.

Firstly, break the argument down by

(a) separating the propositions by numbering them;

(b) putting circles round the words (shown below underlined) that indicate either conclusions (e.g. 'therefore', 'hence', 'so', 'implies') or reasons (e.g. 'since', 'for', 'because', 'assuming'), and

(c) supplying in brackets, the logical indicators that are omitted but clearly suggested.

This first step has been taken in this passage:

'(1) A major challenge posed by the decentralization philosophy is the challenge to lead by persuasion rather than command. (2) This is inherent in the very idea of decentralization, [for] (3) A centralized organization implies control from a central point, with close supervision and issuance of orders, and mandatory courses of action so that (4) the centralized control can be effective. (5) Decentralization, on the other hand, implies freedom for individuals everywhere in the organization to act on the basis of their own knowledge of the particular conditions that apply to the particular problem at hand, [so] (6) In this situation the manager's work is to lead others by drawing out their ideas, their special knowledge and their efforts since (7) self-discipline rather than boss-discipline is the hallmark of a decentralized organization, (8) the manager resorts to command only in emergencies, where he must admit temporary failure to make the situation and the necessary course of action self-evident.

The next step is to set out the statements in the form of a diagram showing the flow of the argument from reasons to conclusions. For example, Fig. 7 is a diagram of the above argument, using numbers to stand for the propositions.

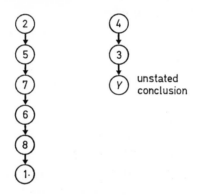

Figure 7

Beardsley argues that reasons for certain conclusions should be grouped close together, and serial arguments should move in one direction to aid clarity. On this basis the argument above is rearranged thus:

'(4) So that centralized control can be effective, (3) a centralized organization controls from a central point with close supervision and issuance of orders, and mandatory courses of action. (Y) Thus command rather than persuasion is appropriate. On the other hand (2) inherent in the very idea of decentralization (5) is freedom for individuals everywhere in the organization to act on the basis of their own knowledge of the particular conditions that apply to the particular problems at hand. (7) Therefore, self-discipline rather than boss-discipline is the hallmark of a decentralized organization. (6) In this situation the manager's work is to lead others by drawing out their ideas, their special knowledge, and their efforts. (8) The manager resorts to command only in emergencies where he must admit temporary failure to make the situation and the necessary course of action self-evident. (1) Therefore, a major challenge posed by the decentralization policy is the challenge to lead by persuasion rather than command.'

Chapter 4

LAWS IN EXPLANATION

Sometimes the word 'law' is used to cover any undisputed fact or empirically established relationship, even though it may be unsupported by other knowledge. Ideally, the term 'law' is reserved for universal propositions related to other laws within some system. Where laws are general they are necessarily abstract as they state a relationship that will always hold under certain stipulated conditions.

Laws may be derived directly from theory, but where they result from observations they may be called 'empirical laws'. An hypothesis may only be concerned with explaining some unique event, while laws are always concerned with explaining *kinds* of events. In certain cases, it is assumed that whenever similar conditions recur, another instance of the event will also occur. Thus, when some hypothesis is established, an explanation of many possible events is also established. Some set of situations is analysed to find the conditions by which they are produced and the universal law implicit in them.

When an hypothesis, that states some general abstract relationship with others is established by being confirmed in many different situations, it comes to be accepted as a law. Usually the original hypothesis has been modified from its original formulation; few hypotheses stand the test of time without some alteration.

CAUSAL RELATIONSHIPS

A law may express a causal relationship; so may an hypothesis explaining some unique event. Consequently it may be asserted, for instance, that the recent high waste level was due to an abnormally high number of trainee workmen who possessed inadequate skill.

Managers cannot anticipate all problems encountered in business management. Unexpected events occur that constitute a problematic situation. There is often a need to find the source of the trouble, that is, to demonstrate how the events making up the problematic situation follow from past events. Like the doctor faced with an epidemic, the manager seeks the cause of the trouble.

The nature of causation is debated. Hume dismissed as an illusion the idea of cause as compelling an effect, and simply viewed cause as an explanation indicating the set of conditions that are present during the occurrence we seek to explain. The dispute still continues, though there is agreement that cause does imply regularity. In science, the word 'cause' is sometimes defined as follows: 'Change C is a cause, if effect E always follows C and if C does not take place, E does not occur.'[1]

In this definition there is a one-to-one relationship between cause and effect; the same cause results in identical effects, and identical effects result from the same cause. The antecedent is always followed by the consequent and this is always preceded by the antecedent. Such a one-to-one relationship is a useful abstraction in teaching science. In practice, the repetition of precisely the same cause is seldom possible and effects cannot usually be specified so precisely that only the one cause is tenable. Hence Feigl suggests a less stringent formulation using 'something like a mathematical limit process'; the more the actual cause approaches the ideal cause, the more the effects will approximate the predicted ideal effects.[2] Even in the physical sciences the strict identity of observed results with those predicted by some law does not occur. The results form a probability distribution. Consequently, laws are provisional in that they are liable to revision as new situations reveal their defects as predictive instruments.

Necessary, Sufficient and Contingent Conditions

1. A factor X may be a *necessary* part of the cause of event Y, in which case Y will not occur unless X occurs. Thus consumer knowledge of a product is a necessary condition for buying that product.
2. Factor X may be a *sufficient* condition for event Y so Y will always occur when X occurs.

[1] Even this definition has its weaknesses. Thus if C = night and E = day, is a causal connection implied?

[2] Herbert Feigl and May Brodbeck (eds), *Readings in the Philosophy of Science*, Appleton-Century-Crofts Inc., New York, 1953, p. 410.

3. Factor X is a *necessary* and *sufficient* condition for event Y if Y always occurs only when X occurs. If X, then always Y. If Y then always X. Only in this case can some result be guaranteed with certainty. This situation can be termed determinate causality.

4. Factor X is a contributory factor to event Y if Y is more likely to happen when X occurs than if X does not occur. A factor may, however, only be contributing under certain contingent conditions; only if A is present will B contribute to producing effect C. Thus if a salesman has high technical expertise (contingent condition) the buyer's liking the salesman (contributory condition) will enhance the probability of a sale being made. There may be alternative contributory conditions dependent on the same contingent condition. For example, if a salesman has high technical expertise (contingent condition), the buyer's liking the salesman or ideological similarity between buyer and seller (alternative contributory conditions) will enhance the probability of a sale being made.

CAUSE IN MANAGEMENT AND THE PHYSICAL AND SOCIAL SCIENCES

Research in the social sciences is mainly concerned with discovering necessary, contributory, and contingent factors. At the very best, they aim at statements of high probability given certain conditions as expressed in the form of 'if A then usually B under conditions XYZ'. For example, job satisfaction is neither necessary nor sufficient to achieve high productivity though it can be a contributory factor. It is for this reason that social scientists like Meehan[1] reject the idea of seeking empirical laws as a basis for deductive explanations. He argues that models can be developed to cope with specific situations and need not be universal in scope. Thus he comments:

'My point here is that the focus on a search for "empirical generalizations" is poor strategy in inquiry since it points the observer in the direction of examining an n of instances rather than concentrating his attention on the essentials of a particular situation.'

[1] Eugene J. Meehan, *Explanation in Social Science: A System Paradigm*, The Dorsey Press, Homewood, Illinois, 1968.

Many historians, too, have been anxious to deny that they are seeking to discover laws that can be used to explain individual events. The historian does not regard the historical event as an instance of a type governed by some law. This is not to deny that generalizations are assumed by historians to be used as a guide in explaining aspects of a unique event. In this sense, the historian is like the manager in seeking to understand the individual situation in all its complexity and is not acting as a scientist in developing and testing theories. The elements in a social situation are often so interrelated and numerous and the situations so varied, that conditions labelled 'stimulus' and any set of results labelled 'response' must necessarily have boundaries that extend beyond their definitions. Repetition of an experiment on the same social group is complicated by effects feeding back to the causal source, thus changing the situation. An experiment adds to people's experience, and this modifies the influence of the same stimulus applied in the future.

Even when control can be established within the laboratory to create precise regularities, they will be no more than probable in the real world because of the inevitable complications of extraneous influences. Under specific laboratory conditions, people can be shown always to avoid painful stimuli, but in real life people will tolerate these to achieve some more important goal.

The solution may appear to lie in devising better measuring techniques. However, we are a long way from developing measurement units for the various social forces to know the number of units of one force that equals a given number of units of another so that net balances can be calculated. An additional problem of measurement lies in determining the effect of combined factors, whether, and to what extent, do they add or subtract from the total effect. As a consequence, laws in social science represent statements that are only probable. Similarly, in history we do not discover cause in the sense defined above, but isolate the conditions attending or contributing to some unique event. When such laws are quoted, we wish to know whether factors are necessary, sufficient, or contributory (and this is often not given, but left to be inferred).

CAUSE IN SCIENCE

As already pointed out, even in the physical sciences, all the necessary and sufficient conditions constituting the cause of some event are seldom given. Hence it is more precise to say that certain antecedents give rise to certain consequents, predictable within statistically defined limits. The 'change' that is labelled 'cause' may begin a process or complete the conditions that collectively ensure the occurrence of an effect.

For most purposes, one can say that the striking of a match caused a fire and take the presence of oxygen, a dry match and a striking surface for granted. Thus, a background of constant conditions necessary for producing the effects is presupposed, and attention is focused on recent significant changes. The health of Churchill was one of the conditions necessary to his success, but it would not normally be included as part of the cause of that success. Thus, a distinction can be made between preconditions and occasioning events. Occasioning events are those that actually bring about the consequences, while preconditions are those events without which the occasioning events would not bring about their effect. Occasioning events are often specific, while preconditions are often not so. Preconditions may take the form of the absence of inhibiting factors in that an event occurs not just because of the push of forces but because counter-forces have been reduced or eliminated.

A law is the rule of inference that links the antecedents to the consequents. The scientist, in a sense, seeks rules that relate antecedent conditions to consequents, hoping eventually to clarify the exact nature of these initial conditions and final effects. Thus, it is not so much that a law, once established, fails in its prediction, but that it is applied inappropriately as the necessary and sufficient antecedents are not present.

Cause is not so much an event as a set of preceding conditions. The idea of cause as a sort of power that produces or compels some specific effects is now rejected. Perhaps the idea of cause as implying compulsion is responsible for emotional attacks on the idea of determinism—that all occurrences are, at least in principle, explicable and predictable. Nagel has pointed out that the assumption of determinism provides stimulus to scientific inquiry, while Kurtz argues that free will can mean no more than that a person's behaviour results partly from his own motives and reasons but that there is a relationship of empirical probability between the set of antecedent biological, psychological and social conditions and the consequent behaviour.

Scientists speak less of cause and effect, than of a causal relationship. They stress the continuity between the set of conditions labelled 'cause' and the set of conditions labelled 'effect', for it is the relationship itself that is of interest and not the properties of the cause. Thus Feigl comments:

'On the whole, the ordinary cause-effect terminology fits best the qualitative macro-level; thus it is part and parcel of the language of commonsense and of those levels of science which deal with gross behaviour and have not as yet introduced quantitative (metrical) concepts. Once measurement is introduced, the gross cause-effect relation gives way to a mathematical formulation in terms of a functional relationship.'[1]

Perhaps functional relationship is even more used by scientists than causal relationship, as it is a less conceptually loaded term. Thus if $Y = X^2$, then Y is a function of X, and X is a function of Y. Both are simply said to be functionally related without assuming any explanatory concepts about necessity or the sequencing of events. The term 'functional dependence' is also used. Thus Y is functionally dependent on X if Y is uniquely determined for each value of X. If a law can be expressed as 'if A then always B', the scientist manipulates A (the independent or active variable) to gauge its effect on B (the dependent variable), e.g. manipulating a financial incentive to gauge its effect on output. He is interested in finding the relationship between A and B. If B is a function of A, we can find a set of ordered pairs showing for each value of A the corresponding value of B. Thus 'if A then always B' can be expressed showing B as a function of A, i.e. $B = f(A)$, which is a rule of correspondence giving the unique value of B for a specific value of A.

Russell is even more condemning of the concept of cause:

'The law of causality, I believe, like much that passes muster among philosophers, is a relic of a bygone age, surviving, like the monarchy, only because it is erroneously supposed to do no harm . . . What I deny is that science assumes the existence of invariable uniformities of sequence of this kind, or that it aims at discovering them . . . There is no question of repetitions of the "same" cause producing the "same" effect; it is not in any

[1] Herbert Feigl and May Brodbeck (eds), *Readings in the Philosophy of Science*, Appleton-Century-Crofts Inc., New York, 1953, p. 410.

sameness of causes and effects that the constancy of scientific law consists, but in sameness of relations. And even "sameness of relations" is too simple a phrase; "sameness of differential equations" is the only correct phrase.'[1]

Whether the causal relationship can be so dismissed or whether its nature still requires explanation is a matter of controversy. Patrick Gardiner[2] argues that to accept Russell's dismissal of the concept of cause would be to accept that the language of physics is the only one that is legitimate.

CAUSE AND CAUSAL CHAINS IN PSYCHOLOGY

The stimulus-response model of behavioural psychology can be interpreted as a cause-and-effect model, though the behavioural response is often regarded as the end of a causal chain so that between the stimulus and the response there is an 'unbroken network of causally related events'. However, we may know simply that S causes R without knowing the intervening causal process by which S produces R. In fact it may not be possible to set out the causal chain and discover the immediate cause. Patrick Gardiner comments along the lines made earlier:

'Which part is the cause? If we answer that the cause is the part directly preceding the effect, that is the final momentary instant before the effect begins, we are then confronted with the difficulty that it is still possible to interpose an infinite number of similar instants between any two selected, and our search for a cause corresponding to the last instant of a process resolves itself into an infinite regress of point events. And thus the use of the causal concept would be impossible.'[3]

The behaviourist approach in psychology was a reaction to the validating of hypotheses by systematic self-reflection which, though perhaps essential in discovering and conceptualizing hypotheses, is insufficient for establishing truth.

The causal process can be shown as a causal chain (Fig. 8).

[1] Bertrand Russell, 'On the Notion of Cause', *Mysticism and Logic and Other Essays*, Allen & Unwin, London, 1917, quoted in H. Feigl and M. Brodbeck, op. cit., pp. 387–95.
[2] Patrick Gardiner, *The Nature of Historical Explanation*, Oxford University Press, London, 1961, pp. 9–10.
[3] Ibid.

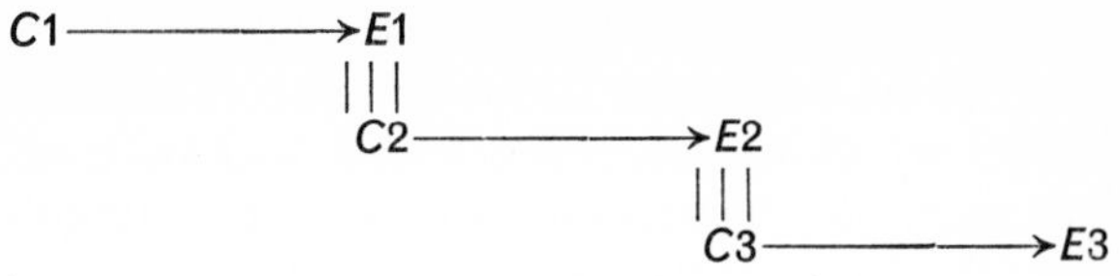

Figure 8

Each cause produces a set of effects, and each set of effects causes another set of effects, and so on. This does not mean that the entire chain must be set out; the level of explanation will depend on the purpose.

CAUSE AS ACTIONABLE CONDITIONS IN MANAGEMENT

If cause does not mean all necessary and sufficient conditions, there must be some criterion for selecting one set of conditions rather than another. What is a causal explanation to one person may be meaningless and useless to another unless it helps him in solving his problem. Thus the cause that is of interest depends on the investigator's purpose.

'The cause of an outbreak of plague may be regarded by the bacteriologist as the microbe he finds in the blood of the victims, by the entomologist as the microbe-carrying fleas that spread the disease, by the epidemiologist as the rats that escaped from the ship and brought the infection into the port.'[1]

This can lead to misunderstanding. One authority claimed that many children were dying of starvation. The government of the country simply quoted the clinical cause of death in terms of specific diseases; no one apparently died of starvation. At a less dramatic level the same sort of debate occurs. Thus managers may be loth to accept that the cause of poor sales was any deficiency in the product itself, and may blame instead the fickleness of the consumer. The conditions chosen as cause are only part of those attendant on the event and are both relevant to the event and to the purpose of the enquiry.

It is all too easy to quote causes reaching so far back that nothing can be done. A manager saying 'that the real cause of petty

[1] W. I. Beveridge, *The Art of Scientific Investigation*, A Vintage Book, 1950, p. 126.

pilfering is the new permissiveness' tells more about the manager's attitude than about how to solve the problem. Causes important to the manager are those human actions or abnormal events which he can counteract or encourage. For example, customers are complaining. The cause of their complaint is the delivery of wrong goods, but such a cause is too general to be actionable. As far as the sales manager is concerned, such a cause is the effect of some other cause, and merely acts as a guide to the discovery of that which is actionable. He may find along the causal chain that there are errors in 'pulling' punch cards as they were wrongly filed—the position is represented diagrammatically in Fig. 9.[1]

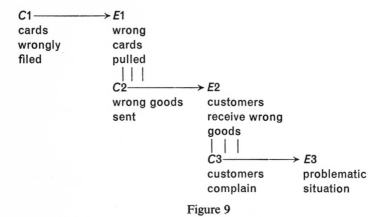

Figure 9

In this case, the effect (customer complaints) has a recognizable cause (customers complain of receiving wrong goods) but this cause needs to be traced back to the actionable cause.

This example demonstrates two points. First, that some so-called 'causes' are simply logical prerequisites—that wrong goods must be sent before wrong goods are received. Second, the length of the causal chain is not fixed; 'customers receive wrong goods' and 'customers complain' could be viewed as the effects of 'wrong goods sent', or the two statements could be separated into cause and effect.

In certain situations, the manager may need to know a more

[1] Diagrams of causal paths can receive much more sophisticated treatment than is indicated in Fig. 9. A technique known as path analysis is one such technique. See E. F. Borgatta (ed), *Sociological Methodology 1969*, Jossey-Bass, San Francisco, 1969, part 1.

immediate cause. Thus, the manager may realize that the night shift produces a higher reject rate than the day shift, but does not know how the two events are connected. The connection might be traced out as in Fig. 10.

The manager traces out the connection, since a regular association between two events is not necessarily one of cause and effect. They may be independent of each other, or both may be the effects of the same common cause. Thus, lower labour turnover in one company division compared with another may be wrongly attributed to differences in personnel policies, when the real reason might be the

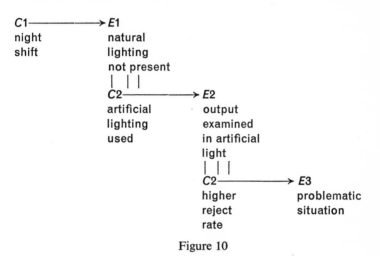

Figure 10

high level of local unemployment. Alternatively, the lower labour turnover and the differences in personnel policies (e.g. more selective testing) may both be the result of one common cause—namely, fewer job opportunities.

Finally, the manager may simply be faced with a set of effects which require explanation. Thus a reduction in sales may have to be explained. The causal chain in this case has to be built up from a detailed analysis of the effects.

It is a common error to assume that what follows an event must be caused by it. It is the most common error made when seeking the cause of the event in retrospect. To avoid this fallacy, a real attempt must be made to eliminate rival hypotheses. Of course, it often happens that when an objection is raised to some 'convenient' hypothesis, a sub- or auxilliary hypothesis is developed to explain it away. Such auxilliary hypotheses can always be developed. This is common in social science papers to explain why an hypothesis was not confirmed. In fact, more imagination may be put into explaining away awkward findings than in developing the original hypothesis.

The fallacy of confusing cause with antecedent (*post hoc, ergo propter hoc*) is common among management explanations. One company director was convinced that a fall off in sales occurring after heaters were put in salesmen's cars resulted from salesmen being too 'snug' to leave them and sell, and he refused to entertain more probable explanations. Another confusion of cause with a non-causal antecedent occurs when a new system is regarded as the cause of some subsequent event, whereas the cause lies in the removal of the old system. Consequently, technological change may appear to cause subsequent labour troubles when the difficulty results from the management ignoring certain social relationships when introducing the new technology.

Even where there appears to be an obvious relationship of cause and effect, the two factors may interact with each other in such a way that neither can be said to cause the other. For example, does the nature of language determine what can be thought, or does thought determine the nature of language? Each may affect the other. Similarly attitudes are said to affect behaviour, but in practice behaviour can also change attitudes. Interacting systems are sometimes ignored by social scientists and a simple cause-and-effect system is assumed. Thus McGregor writes:

'The social scientist does not deny that human behaviour in industrial organization today is approximately what management perceives it to be. He has, in fact, observed it and studied it fairly extensively. But he is pretty sure that this behaviour is not a consequence of man's inherent nature. It is a consequence rather of the nature of industrial organizations, of management philosophy, policy, and practice. The conventional approach of theory X is based on mistaken notions of what is cause and what is effect.'[1]

This is the fallacy of simplism; both management practices and people's behaviour modify and affect each other. The S-O-R

[1] C. J. Haberstroh and A. H. Rubinstein, *Some Theories of Organization*, The Dorsey Press & Richard Irwin, Homewood, Illinois, 1960, p. 179.

(Stimulus-Organism-Response) model when viewed as a dynamic model forms an interacting system, as there is usually feedback from the response to the source of the stimulus which in turn modifies the stimulus. At a more mundane level, the assumption in many training programmes for salesmen is that the result of the sales interview depends on the salesman. It should be recognized that his performance is also affected by the behaviour of the buyer, so that the outcome is affected by their mutual interaction.

Finally, much time can be spent in determining the cause of some variation, when the variation is a likely chance fluctuation. In practice, the effects from some cause may only be predicted to within certain chance limits of error. Thus the same machine does not produce identical units, though they may be regarded as such for the purpose of sale.

For practical purposes, there is a one-to-many relationship between cause and effect; a particular cause results in a range of possible effects. To explain in detail the cause of a particular effect would require the manager to consider many chance contingencies, each altering the effect so slightly that explaining all of them would be neither possible nor worth while. The science of statistics lets the manager take account of this by assigning limits between which chance fluctuations in effects probably lie with a specified degree of likelihood. Thus, whenever the manager is faced with variation in the results emanating from supposedly common processing, the chance of this happening should first be calculated to establish whether it is worth while seeking some assignable cause.

The question is 'How does the manager fill in the appropriate links in the causal chain?' There are three stages in isolating a cause:

(a) having the right concept of possible causes;
(b) selecting the most plausible cause in which action may be taken; and
(c) verifying the cause.

Having the Right Concepts as to Possible Cause

Logic and the philosophy of science give no guidance to the formation of a list of possible actionable causes. There is no certain way of deducing causes from effects or even effects from causes. It is argued that insight into the discovery of probable causes is a matter for

73

psychology, not scientific method. One cannot build an algorithm, or routine procedure, for discovering causes. What seems to be required is appropriate experience of the system under study and ingenuity in using analogies. One error is to assume that effects and causes must be of a similar nature, e.g. that a sudden sensitivity to price must result from a fall-off in incomes.

If a person does not have a mental store of possible causes that includes the correct one, he cannot discover the cause. If Robinson Crusoe had found the print of an animal he had never seen, there are strict limits to what he could have deduced from the print. Again, a layman has little skill in determining the clinical cause of death; nor would he know which effects were relevant to the cause, unless the body was mutilated or visibly abnormal. The inexperienced layman does not discover why his car engine has failed, though he may look for disconnected parts knowing that they must be connected to work; unless a man has some background mechanical knowledge, he simply does not know what to look for in trying to understand the relationships between the parts of the engine, for the idea that X might be the cause of Y is only tenable against some background idea of why this might be so.

When cause is confused with some non-causal antecedent event, attempts are usually made to justify this belief with reasons. In analysing effects, a person may not recall explicitly any basic theory, but some knowledge is an indispensable part of his search. In fact, the terms used in describing each link in the causal chain are usually 'theory loaded', suggesting why the link is feasible.

What has the psychologist to offer? To the psychologist, the ability to find causes is a *diagnostic* skill. He would agree with the philosopher that moving back to cause assumes knowledge concerning possible causes; each link in the causal chain represents a diagnosis. Thus even Robinson Crusoe would begin, after viewing the print in the sand, with the idea that some living thing had caused it and then, on examining the print further, would deduce that only a human could have made that exact impression. Both of these deductions assume concepts about cause. The more experienced a person is, the more concepts he will have of possible causes. Concepts enable the individual to generalize his experience to a variety of analogous situations.

Few problematic situations facing a manager result from causes that would never occur to him, though he might dismiss such causes as improbable. Furthermore, many problems which face a manager recur and are inherent in the job. Thus a fall-off in sales is a frequent concern of the sales manager; labour recruitment difficulties go with the job of personnel; machine breakdowns go with the job of maintenance engineer; getting out figures in time goes with the job of the accountant; increase in wastage levels, reduction in quality, and labour disputes go with the job of the production manager; and the sudden outbreak of fires is the problem facing the fire chief. The aim of each of these people should be to systematize his knowledge into a hierarchy of possible causes of such situations. Thus the fire chief might erect a complex of causes as shown in Fig. 11. Of course, the resulting problem might be a combination of causal factors, but the main thing is for each problem-solver to 'know what can go wrong' and to have a store of possible causal explanations.

Even the outsider has ideas of the cause of many problems that arise in industry, as he possesses many concepts, developed in day-to-day living, which can be generalized to the new problem situation found in business. However, his store of ideas is likely to be limited. For example, if we asked a trainee the probable cause of wrong goods being sent out, he might well say simply that someone had made an error and be able to proceed no further. If we asked him the cause of the increased reject rate on the night shift, 'common sense' might suggest to him that supervision was being more lax. But in both cases the experienced supervisor would be able to recall from his knowledge of the processes involved and his past experience, a greater number of possible causes.

Selecting the Most Plausible Cause for Action

A number of philosophers have argued for a 'logic of discovery', that would at least generate 'plausible conjectures' for entertaining one particular set of conditions rather than another as the likely cause of some event. In other words, are there any grounds for believing some hypothesis is more probable than its rivals without resort to testing?

There are several reasons for regarding one actionable causal hypothesis as more likely than its rival. One may simply rely on past observation. The manager recalls the occurrence of some past events that could possibly be the cause. As no other 'relevant' past events occur to him, he assumes this to be the most likely cause; but we have seen there is an inherent danger in this procedure. Another method is that of 'trial and error' used by the technician. This assumes that the situation can be reproduced and factors varied at will. Such a method is not generally available to

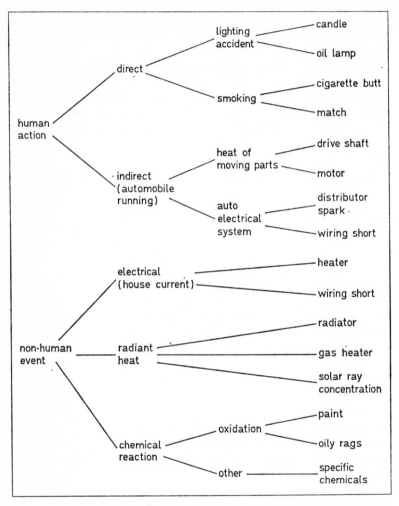

Figure 11. 'A possible hierarchical arrangement of concepts applicable to the cause of fires' (from Psychology and Human Performance: An Introduction to Psychology by Robert M. Gagne and Edwin A. Fleishman. Copyright © 1959 by Holt, Rinehart & G. Winston, Inc. reprinted by permission of Holt, Rinehart & Winston, Inc.).

the manager, as the nature of the situation precludes experiment. He is faced with a set of effects, and must proceed from there. These effects usually appear to have many possible causes.

There seems to be a many-to-one relationship between cause and effect, just as there are many causes of death. However, a doctor on examining a body will usually give a specific cause of death (other than heart failure!) based on his extensive knowledge of the physical effects of various causal agencies. Although it may be true to say 'each different kind of cause produces some difference in effects and each different effect is produced by some difference in cause' we cannot always distinguish between the effects of different causes, or deduce which causes are associated with which effects. In spite of this, an analysis of effects can rule out a whole class of causes that otherwise might be suspected.

We can take the earlier example of complaints about the sending of wrong goods. The increase in the number of complaints was a recent event and, therefore, we can assume that 'something has gone wrong or more wrong'. Analysis of the orders sent out might reveal:

1. The order advice notes 'check with the goods in the parcels'. This rules out 'wrong goods packed'. Addresses on the parcels agree with the addresses on the orders. This rules out 'right goods packed to the wrong account' but not necessarily 'right goods packed to the wrong address'.
2. The original order from the representative does not coincide with the processed order sent. This tends to rule out the representative, and suggests that the error lies in order-processing.

Thus the manager needs to analyse effects, but what effects? A complete description of all effects would be impossible. Also, some effects are irrelevant to the problem at hand. The manner in which customers complain would be irrelevant to discovering how the error arose, though it might be relevant in determining the urgency of the problem. The actionable cause is that set of causal antecedents the manager can alter. The cause must be not only a necessary or significant contributory factor in producing what has occurred, but also important to the manager from the point of view of his responsibilities.

A problematic situation is a deviation from the expected or the customary. This 'abnormality' is explained by some prior 'abnormality' in events or actions of people which, from the standpoint of the manager, is a condition he can do something to correct. Even where cause and effect are interacting, the factor that is labelled 'cause' is that which can be more easily controlled. Thus it is debatable whether apathetic subordinates, with low output and unable to take initiative or accept responsibilities, reflect management practices, or whether the type of management is the result of apathetic subordinates. However, in selecting management as the cause, top management is indicating that it is easier to change supervision than to alter directly the attitudes of subordinates.

We have already pointed out that a person completely ignorant of possible causes would not know which effects were relevant and which were not. Assuming that the manager has a store of concepts

Table 1

Order	Probability of solution 1st attempt	Probability of solution 2nd attempt
XYZ	0·7	0·9
XZY	0·7	0·8
YXZ	0·2	0·9
YZX	0·2	0·3
ZXY	0·1	0·8
ZYX	0·1	0·3

about cause that includes the true one, he can analyse them to select that cause which best fits the effects. But he may still come out with several possible causes. Which does he investigate first? He should consider first the cause which in his experience and that of his colleagues has most frequently been associated with the effects in question. This cause is normally the one to investigate first, though occasionally the time and cost needed to investigate some other cause may be so trivial that it might be given priority.

We can illustrate this further. Suppose that the possible causes would be X, Y or Z and that past experience indicates roughly that on 7 out of 10 occasions it is X, on 2 out of 10 occasions it is Y, and on 1 out of 10 it is Z. If the manager chooses to investigate X as the most likely causal agent, then Y and finally Z, on all occasions that he is presented with the effects he will eventually be more efficient in finding cause (Table 1).

Of course, in this example, the cause must be found by the third attempt, as there are only three possible causes. But, the important point is this: the manager who selects causes for testing in order of their probability is likely to solve the problem in the shortest time.

It is suggested that we select the most probable hypothesis from a range of possible ones. Popper argues for the opposite. Of hypotheses that remain open, he argues that we should select the one that is least probable, as an hypothesis of low probability is more easily falsified and hence more corroborated if it withstands testing. The content of an hypothesis increases with its falsifiability: the more falsifiable an hypothesis seems, the more potentially informative it is. Probability and factual content are inversely related; the more we gamble on the truth of an hypothesis, the greater is the potential reward.

Although certain propositions are obvious when stated, they may still have useful content, since 'perhaps more people fail by ignoring the obvious than by failing to penetrate the obscure'. If one takes Berelson and Steiner's book[1] *Human Behaviour: An Inventory of Scientific Findings* as indicative of the findings of sociology, then few of the propositions found there are counter-intuitive, and time might have been wasted in seeking counter-intuitive hypotheses. At least in social science, economy of effort seems to dictate the testing of the more probable hypothesis: time being devoted to establishing the relative importance of variables and the universality of propositions. Again, as we have shown, to select the most probable hypothesis can save time. In fact, deliberately to choose the least probable hypothesis would, for the manager, mean that he should ignore what experience has taught him. Levi also makes the following comment:

'Hypotheses that are false but are highly amenable to rigorous testing are abundantly available. What is more, hypotheses that are false but survive rigorous testing are also far from lacking.'[2]

Popper uses the term 'corroboration' rather than 'confirmation' of hypothesis, as the word 'confirmation' suggests that truth has been established. He argues that his method is purely deductive. However, with the introduction of the concept of corroboration, it is reasonable to argue that the deductivism of Popper is a form of induction.

[1] B. Berelson and G. A. Steiner, *Human Behaviour: An Inventory of Scientific Findings*, Harcourt, Brace & World Inc., New York, 1964.
[2] Isaac Levi, *Gambling with Truth*, Borzoi Books, 1967, p. 110.

Verifying the Cause

The testing of causal hypotheses in a scientific way may be direct or indirect. Where the phenomenon can be directly manipulated, the testing follows the laboratory-type experiment where factors can be introduced, removed and varied at will. Where the phenomenon is not open to direct manipulation but can be directly observed then by observing different states and contrasting situations, it may be possible to isolate the actionable cause. These and other methods are described below. All are variations of the hypothetico-deductive method already described. The hypothesis is first formulated as a result of an interplay between observation and experience, and its consequences are deduced and tested as conforming to empirical fact.

Any possible cause is merely an hypothesis until checked, and simply indicates 'what to look for' in order to verify. If A is the cause of B then S and T will be found, S and T being the consequences that follow if A is the cause. The process of verification consists of confirming that S and T are in accordance with expectations. In other words, (i) if predictions based on the hypothetical cause are consistently confirmed or all failures in this can be understood to be the result of contingencies that could not be avoided, and (ii) if no other hypotheses can account for the consequences with greater simplicity, then the hypothesis is accepted tentatively as probable. The main fallacy to avoid is concluding that B was caused by A just because B followed A. The manager cannot usually undertake the sort of controlled experiment conducted in science to protect himself against such error.

A problem arises when some results are as predicted by the hypothesis and others are not. Thus we may formulate the hypothesis that the presence of an observer results in an improvement in individual output. In testing the hypothesis, we find that sometimes the presence of an observer does improve the performance and sometimes does not. We may be tempted to abandon the hypothesis. However, if we persist (as some research workers did) and contrast the subjects affected negatively with those who are affected positively, we may find that for those affected positively the job being done is already well learnt, but that it is still new to those affected negatively. Our original hypothesis is then modified to become 'the presence of an observer increases performance on a task already well learnt but inhibits the learning of new skills'. Even this hypothesis may have to be modified for sharper prediction, and so we may allow for different types of observer, to distinguish, say, between a trainer and other types of observer. Such is the way knowledge progresses—from broad generalities to deterministic answers.

Psychologists argue that the most successful practical problem-solvers are those who pay particular attention to verification. There is a strong tendency to regard a problem as solved when a cause is found that fits the effects because of a natural desire to be rid of the problem. It is all too easy to select evidence favourable to some attractive hypothesis and to ignore the collection of evidence that might be unfavourable. In this respect, research students are notorious for getting results that always seem to corroborate the beliefs of their professors. The aim in confirming an hypothesis is to seek evidence that is most likely to test it severely.

In some cases it is impossible to show the probable cause except by taking appropriate action and confirming that the problem has been alleviated. If a change in the presumed cause has an appreciable influence on the effects, when other presumed causes remain unchanged, then at least the manager can say that he has uncovered some of the significant conditions. But even then the real causal factors may remain unspecified. Take for example one study in job enlargement; the aim was to design jobs so that the worker performed a larger sequence and wider variety of tasks. It resulted in a twenty per cent increase in output, and this was attributed to the psychological consequences of job enlargement. Subsequently an industrial engineer showed that the original specialization resulted in bottle-necks and poor team-balancing, and that job enlargement could have accounted for the increase in output simply by eliminating enforced idleness. We should only accept a presumed cause after we have made every effort to disprove it.

LABORATORY-TYPE EXPERIMENTATION

If cause were interpreted as 'all necessary and sufficient conditions to produce the effect', two consequences would logically follow from any causal hypothesis if it were true:

1. The events B, whose cause is to be explained, must be present if the alleged cause A is present, i.e. if A, always B.

F

2. The alleged cause *A* must have been present when the events *B* whose cause is to be explained, occurred, i.e. if *B*, always *A*.

It is this concept of cause that lies behind the 'five canons' of inductive inquiry which were believed to be methods for both discovering and establishing causes. They were popularized by the nineteenth-century English philosopher John Stuart Mill. Though they were developed originally by John Herschel, they have come to be known as 'Mill's canons'. In fact, Mill's canons were neither methods of proof nor methods of discovery, being based on a view of causation that regards nature as being conveniently divided into separable parts. However, they form useful tests if we remember that even a law is never absolutely proved, and that demanding certainty is demanding 'a guarantee where it is logically impossible to obtain one'. Thus Feigl comments:

> 'The identification of causes (or causal factors) proceeds most reliably by the experimental and statistical methods. The canons of experimental inquiry and formulated by J. S. Mill (while never sufficient as definitive proofs of causation, may establish at least some inductive probabilities) can be generalized and refined for the field of statistical regularities (correlation theory and factor analysis). The usual difficulties encountered here are the "plurality of causes", the "ignored concomitant causal conditions", etc. These difficulties make up the major concern of causal (etiological, prognosticative) research in the empirical sciences.'[1]

Mill's Canons

1. The method of agreement. Mill's statement of this canon is as follows:

> 'If two or more instances of the phenomenon under investigation have only one circumstance in common, the circumstance in which alone all the instances agree is the cause or effect, or an indispensable part of the cause, of the given phenomenon.'

Thus the canon argues that if

$$AB \text{ precedes } E$$
$$AC \text{ precedes } E$$
$$AD \text{ precedes } E$$

[1] Herbert Feigl and May Brodbeck (eds), *Readings in the Philosophy of Science*, Appleton-Century-Crofts Inc., New York, 1953, p. 417.

then A, being the factor common in all three instances, is causally connected to E.

2. The joint method of agreement and differences.

'If two or more instances in which the phenomenon occurs have only one circumstance in common, while two or more instances in which it does not occur have nothing in common save the absence of that circumstance, the circumstance in which alone the two sets of instances differ is the cause or the effect or an indispensable part of the cause of the phenomenon.'

3. The method of difference.

'If an instance in which the phenomenon under investigation occurs and an instance in which it does not occur have every circumstance in common save one, that one occurring in the former, the circumstance in which alone the two instances differ is the cause or an indispensable part of the cause of the phenomenon.'

Thus the method of difference argues that if

$$AB \text{ precedes } E$$
$$\bar{A}B \text{ precedes } \bar{E}$$

(where $\bar{A}$ or $\bar{E}$ indicates their absence), then there is a causal relationship between A and E. The method is reflected in the use of both an experimental group (to which stimulus A is applied) and a control group (to which no stimulus is applied) in the design of experiments.

4. The method of concomitant variations.

'Whatever phenomenon varies in any manner whenever another phenomenon varies in some particular manner, is either a cause or an effect of that phenomenon, or is connected with it through some fact of causation.'

5. The method of residues.

'Subduct from any phenomenon such part as is known by previous inductions to be the effect of certain antecedents, and the residue of the phenomenon is the effect of the remaining antecedents.'

The method of agreement depends on having a number of instances that are different in all respects but one. It attempts to establish that *A* is a sufficient condition for *E*. Thus if a manager employed a supervisor in a number of different sections and on each occasion labour turnover increased and labour troubles occurred, the manager might conclude the supervisor was to blame. The limitations to the method are apparent. There is difficulty in ensuring agreement in only one respect and the method cannot distinguish between causation and co-existence. We can never be sure, for example, that some additional factor is not also at work in each situation to which the supervisor was moved.

The joint method of agreement and difference brings in negative instances together with the positive. It tries to establish both necessary and sufficient conditions for event *E*. Thus, in our example it might have been confirmed that there was no labour trouble in sections of the factory where the supervisor was absent.

The method of difference requires instances that are alike in all respects except one. It attempts to establish a necessary condition for *E* to occur. Thus a manager notes an increase in yarn breakages. The men, the machines, atmospheric conditions, are all the same but the yarn is being supplied by a new supplier. The manager might conclude that the new supplier's yarn is to blame.

A common reflection of the method is seen when identical units are set up for control purposes. Whether such units are shops in a multiple chain or typing-pools in a firm, their similarity allows direct comparison and is an aid in isolating reasons for differences in performance. The difficulty in this method lies in ensuring that only one change at a time is made, and that the situation into which the change is introduced remains the same.

The method of concomitant variation assesses the variation between factors that may be causally related. It suggests causation by establishing a linear correlation between the independent variable (the 'cause') and the dependent variable (the 'effect'). It is common to calculate an index of the relationship (a correlation coefficient) as a statistical measure of association between the two variables. In fact, such correlation does not establish a causal connection; both elements may be the effects of some third, undiscovered, element, or the high linear correlation may be chance. However, the method is useful in supplying lines for further investigation. Consequently, if smoking and lung cancer are causally related, then one consequence of this would be a correlation between the extent of smoking and lung cancer not explicable by chance.

An executive is constantly looking for similar relationships, as a basis for prediction. For example, if he knows that sales of his product have in the past changed with predicted population shifts, he can use such conditions to forecast his own sales. No assumptions need be made about causal relationships. Or he may note the relationship between calling rates of salesmen and resulting sales. There is a danger, when a relationship is found within certain limits, of extrapolating outside them. For example, within limits, there will be a relationship between the amount of work done and the number of hours worked. In the belief that such a relationship holds indefinitely, the executive might decide to allow such excessive overtime that less is gained in output than would have been obtained with fewer hours of work.

The method of residues is not a distinct method but is supplemental to the others, and depends on having explained some of the events already. The manager might explain a reduction in sales by pointing out that X per cent is accounted for as a result of discontinuing to sell a particular line and Y per cent as a result of losing certain accounts, so the remainder can be accounted for by the only other factor in the situation, namely the weather.

Modern statistical techniques, while showing Mill's formulation to be naive, have in reality compensated for many deficiencies of the canons. Both the method of difference and agreement assume the presence or absence of E rather than changes in the degree to which E can be present. Analysis of variance is the modern statistical approach to experiments, and it takes into account that E could vary by degrees, that several factors may affect E, and that the effect of each one on E needs to be estimated. It also recognizes that all conditions cannot be controlled, so chance plays a part in determining E. Thus Kaplan comments as follows on the methodology suggested by Mill's canons:

'The obvious difficulty with this one-factor theory, already recognized in its classic formulations, is its assumption that the various conditions are independent . . . Even when the assumption of independence is not made, we are usually not in a position to say how the several factors are dependent on one another, and especially not in a position to say that their covariation is expressible by some simple function . . . The mathematics and statistics of the eighteenth and nineteenth centuries could conveniently manage only two changing variables at a time, and the ideal experiment was therefore conceived as an experiment in which all the variables but two were held constant. One, the "independent variable" was then manipulated, while observations were made on the other, the "dependent variable". This was the practical basis of the classical one-factor theory of experiment mentioned in the preceding section. But contemporary mathematics no longer imposes this constraint, and manipulation, whether to hold "everything else" constant, or to introduce changes in the one factor is correspondingly no longer absolutely essential.'[1]

Kaplan also points out that experiment has a number of purposes other than seeking causal relationships:

1. Methodological experiment, where the aim is to develop the techniques being used.
2. Heuristic experiment, where the aim is merely to stimulate ideas for further inquiry.
3. Clarification experiment, where the aim is to clarify some concept or determine the magnitude of some factor.
4. Boundary experiment, to discover the limits which apply to some law.
5. Simulation experiment, using some model to find out what would happen in the real world as suggested from manipulation of the model.

[1] Abraham Kaplan, *The Conduct of Inquiry: Methodology for Behavioral Science*, Chandler Publishing Co., San Francisco, pp. 158–62.

Chapter 5

BEHAVIOURAL RESEARCH

EXPERIMENTATION WITH PEOPLE

Experiment is controlled observation. The investigator manipulates an independent variable, and gauges its effect. He tries to control the situation, so that variation between stimulus and response (independent and dependent variable) other than that caused by the stimulus, is minimized. The experiment contrasts with the *ex post facto* type of analysis dealt with up to now, where we are trying in retrospect to discover functional relationships or relationships between antecedents and their consequents. As the opportunity is seldom present in management decision-making for controlling and manipulating a variable, experiment is not common in management research.

Table 2

	Observer is participant	Observer is non-participant
Nature of experiment known to subjects	X	X
Nature of experiment not known to subjects	X	X

In experiments with people, the observer may or may not reveal the nature or even the fact of his experiment to those subjected to it. Hence we have the matrix of possible situations shown in Table 2.

Experiments with people require special precautions resulting from the problems of control and measurement. In establishing by experiment that stimulus S is the cause of behaviour-response R in any group G, it is necessary to subject G to treatment S. S can be regarded as the independent variable, and R as the dependent variable. Expressed graphically, the horizontal X axis would be the independent variable and the vertical Y axis the dependent variable. The problem is one of ensuring that the exact response of group G to S is accurately calculated since the outcome after applying

S to G is influenced by (i) other contemporary events affecting G during the time span of the experiment; (ii) the possibility that group G may change its relevant characteristics during the period of the experiment; (iii) the introduction of bias by the experimental process itself because people are aware of being tested; (iv) possible bias of behaviour by the initial measurement of the state of group G, where it is necessary to do this.

These factors could bias the result by giving rise to extraneous variance that is systematic. One way round this problem is to set up two homogeneous groups for comparison purposes and to assign subjects at random to them. One group constitutes the experimental group and is subjected to S, while the other constitutes the control group and is not subjected to treatment S, unless the two groups function alternately in a control and experimental capacity. Alternatively, we may set up two groups deliberately matched on the factors

Table 3

	Pre-experiment state	Post-experiment state
Experimental group	$E1$	$E2$
Control group	$G1$	$G2$

considered relevant to the experimental outcome, by first listing matched pairs of subjects, then taking members of each pair and allocating them at random between an experimental and a control group. Of course the two groups may simply have to be chosen on the basis of judgment, as occurs when a city is divided into zones for promotion-testing purposes.

The measurement of response-behaviour R would be the difference between the condition of the control and experimental groups at the end of the experiment in respect of the relevant characteristics (Table 3).

Thus the effect of S is $(E2-G2)$ on the assumption that $E1$ and $G1$ are in identical states from the point of view of the experiment. In circumstances where such perfectly matched groups are not possible, the effect of S is

$$(E2-G2)-(E1-G1) = (E2-E1)-(G2-G1)$$

For example, if some stimulus S (e.g. new method of operator-training) is intended to increase a group's score on an attainment test, then allowance must be made for the fact that the state of $E1$ and $G1$ are not identical.

Score

$$E1 = 115$$
$$G1 = 110$$
$$E2 = 120$$
$$G2 = 110$$

Thus the effect of S could be $(120-110)-(115-110) = 5$, if we ignored the role of chance error.

The above analysis ignores the possibility that differences between scores have arisen purely by chance. The process in statistics known as 'significance testing' is concerned with determining whether the difference between measures could result from chance.

Where more than two groups are involved, the appropriate statistical technique is the 'analysis of variance'.[1] It can be used to analyse observed differences between more than two sample statistics to determine whether the observed differences could be attributed to chance. The technique is also used to estimate the part of the difference (or variance) due to experimental treatment and that due to other factors.

Factorial analysis of variance allows us to manipulate two or more variables or factors at the same time. Thus we can gauge the effect of several independent variables upon some dependent variable. For example, we could allow for the additional variable of 'sex' in the illustration above, thus measuring its effect rather than minimizing or eliminating its effect by matching or considering groups of only one sex (Fig. 12).

For the crossbreak below we could, as a consequence of factorial analysis of variance, test for the significance of the difference between

(*a*) old and new methods of training,
(*b*) male and female scores, and
(*c*) methods and sex of subject (since the new method may work better with one sex than the other).

The 'factorial' design includes all combinations of the factors. Where $n = $ the number of factors and there are two levels of each factor, there would be 2^n combinations. (There are $2^2 = 4$ cells in

[1] Analysis of variance is the correct technique for two groups also; the t-test is a special case of the analysis of variance.

the crossbreak below). However, there may be practical difficulties in dealing with more than four independent variables, i.e. $2^4 = 16$ combinations.

We may wish to gauge the effect of several stimuli on several different groups. For example, we may wish to assess the relative effectiveness of (say) four different point-of-sale aids, A, B, C and D, on store sales. If we tried out each of the four in four different

<table>
<tr><td></td><td></td><td colspan="2" align="center">A
(training given)</td><td></td></tr>
<tr><td></td><td></td><td align="center">A_1</td><td align="center">A_2</td><td></td></tr>
<tr><td rowspan="2">B
(sex)</td><td>B_1
(male)</td><td>(new training)
E_2
(male)</td><td>(training
unchanged)
G_2
(male)</td><td>(note: two
levels of each
factor A_1 A_2
and B_1 B_2)</td></tr>
<tr><td>B_2
(female)</td><td>E_2
(female)</td><td>G_2
(female)</td><td></td></tr>
</table>

Figure 12

towns, the difference in results could be due to the town. Another source of systematic variance could be the socio-economic variable of the clientele. A latin square design (Fig. 13), is one way of coping with such systematic variance. Each of the four different point-of-sale aids A, B, C and D is tried in each of towns 1, 2, 3 and 4 for each of socio-economic groups I, II, III and IV.

		Town			
		1	2	3	4
Socio-economic level of clientele	I.	D	A	B	C
	II	C	D	A	B
	III	B	C	D	A
	IV	A	B	C	D

Figure 13

Again, the results will be analysed by analysis of variance.

Where there is the danger of the experimental process in itself biasing the results, the process of the experiment is also repeated with the control group, e.g. a placebo is given to the control group.

There are a number of other reasons additional to that given for measuring the state of the relevant characteristics before as well as after the experiment. It may be a prerequisite to selecting matched groups, where purely random methods of selection may be inadequate. Also the initial state of some group may rule out the experiment; for example, morale may be so high that further efforts to stimulate it would be futile. Furthermore we may wish to measure the net change as a result of the experiment. But a change from an initial level of (say) 20% awareness to 40% constitutes a 100% change, while a change from 40% to 60% would tend to be regarded as only a 50% change. This can be misleading and hence social scientists use as a measure, not the percentage increase, but the net increase in percentage divided by the maximum increase possible. Thus if X represents the initial (pre-experiment) percentage and Y the final (post-experiment) percentage, the effectiveness index[1] is

$$\frac{Y-X}{100-X}$$

Comparing the two cases above,

Initial percentage $= 20\%$,

Final percentage $= 40\%$,

Effectiveness index $= \dfrac{40-20}{100-20} = \dfrac{20}{80}$

$= 25\%$,

whereas

Initial percentage $= 40\%$,

Final percentage $= 60\%$,

Effectiveness index $= \dfrac{60-40}{100-40} = \dfrac{20}{60}$

$= 33\frac{1}{3}\%$.

[1] See P. F. Lazarsfeld in *The Language of Social Research*, ed. Paul F. Lazarsfeld and Morris Rosenberg, The Free Press, New York, and Collier-Macmillan Ltd., London, ch. 11.

Finally, it may be desirable to know the way R varies with different amounts of S, and this is a further reason for pre-experiment measurement.

Initial measurement always introduces the possibility of bias. To overcome this problem, additional control groups may be introduced. For example, the first control group is not subjected to S, but is still measured before and after the experiment, while the second is subjected to S, but measured only after the experiment.

PROBLEM OF EXTERNAL VALIDITY

The above precautions are to ensure internal validity—that is, ensuring that R did in fact occur as a result of treatment S, and not by chance. But there is also the problem of external validity— whether the results can be generalized. To what extent can the results be generalized on the assumption that the conditions of a valid experiment have been met? For the results to apply to population ABC, the control and experimental groups need to be representative samples. People from different regions and cultures may react differently to some particular stimulus, whether it is an advertisement, a method of supervisory behaviour or simply a shorter working week. Only after experiments are repeated, using different groups which are shown to respond similarly, can we be justified in generalization.

The problem of external validity is a major one. Experiments in industry can never be based on random samples of the working population. Unless there is other evidence to justify generalization to other populations, conclusions from the experiment should be restricted to those on whom the experiment was carried out. Yet generalizations are usually illicitly made. Thus for years it was taken for granted that informal work groups at the shop floor level were patterned after those shown to exist at the Hawthorne plant of the Western Electricity Company in the US. This gave rise to a great deal of advice by social scientists to management. Only in recent years, following work by such people as Crozier in France, has the pattern been shown to be by no means universal.

The complexity of experimenting with people can be better understood if we recognize that the response of some subject is tied to a particular object, and occurs within some specific context. A change in context can affect both the response and the object to which the response is directed. Yet the aspects of the context relevant to producing some result can form a major part of the research project.

There is the further problem of size: the extent to which regularities established at a micro-level are applicable to more macro-systems. Small systems may not be isomorphic models of the larger system, so that extrapolation may be wrong. Similarly, what has been established at the macro-level may not apply at the level of the individual unit. As the research psychologist moves (along a continuum?) from the individual to the primary group, to secondary groups and so on, there is a need to establish both the nature of the link and the new or modified variables that arise as a result of increasing the unit of inquiry.

Determining the inferences to be drawn from an experiment is a highly complex matter. It may be foolish to generalize, as we have seen, from one particular experiment, if this runs counter to what experience has previously suggested. Yet we find social scientists dismissing the views of industrial consultants and others as not based on hard evidence, when their own counter-view is based on one or two experiments in highly artificial situations.

But the irritation of social scientists with current beliefs is understandable. Management, in seeking quick solutions to complex problems, fall for the slogan, the 'potted' thinking, to make into routine what would otherwise take time and require disciplined mental effort. It is sad to reflect how few managers have heard of Herbert Simon as a leading management academic, yet the slogans of authors who substitute one half-truth for another are constantly repeated. For example, it is argued that executives rise one step above the job they can do most competently. It can equally be argued that there are too many artificial barriers keeping people in jobs well below that for which their ability fits them. There are more plausible rival hypotheses (associated with the growth in management techniques) to account for the greater part of growth in the administrative side of government and business, running counter to the hypothesis which states that this arises from work expanding to fill the time available to do it.

This is not to suggest that these new half-truths serve no purpose. On the contrary they can stimulate the search for new courses of action. The real objection lies in treating them as having any particular scientific merit. However, the popular fallacies are as common among management as in the population at large: the appeal to tradition in saying it is tried and, therefore, true; damning the source of an idea instead of judging the idea itself; appeal to authority that is not an expert witness as sufficient in itself; attacking the man and not the argument ('We all know he's ambitious'); the cultural fallacy ('hardly British'); and so on.

FIELD EXPERIMENTS, FIELD STUDIES AND NATURAL EXPERIMENTS

We have discussed experimentation both in the laboratory and in the field. In general, more control can be exercised within the laboratory, so that testing relationships is easier though the situation is artificial and may be far removed from everyday life. The laboratory experiment may fabricate situations which do not appear in real life, i.e. their external validity is often in question. Thus attitudes may be easy to change in a laboratory situation, but difficult elsewhere. Although in a field experiment the researcher seeks to manipulate and control, there is usually some contamination of his results as less control is possible. Field experiments are often used as a follow-up to laboratory experiments to test their significance in the real world. For example, there have been field experiments in which supervisory behaviour was manipulated to gauge the effect on labour productivity. They must be distinguished from natural experiments and field studies.

In the natural experiment, changes are not initiated by the researcher but by others; there is generally no control group and the researcher seeks to establish relationships while observing the process. Establishing such relationships between dependent and independent variables generally requires statistical techniques. Karl Pearson was the first to develop a measure for the relationship between two variables known as the 'correlation coefficient'. There is also a rank 'correlation coefficient' which is a measure of association between two rank variables after the variables have been ranked in ascending or descending order of value. Of increasing importance is multiple regression which is the relationship between a dependent variable and a set of independent variables.

Although a field study is concerned with a real life situation, it is *ex post facto*: the investigator may attempt to test hypotheses and establish relationships, or alternatively his investigation may be only exploratory.

94

Interrogation

All data cannot be obtained by observation, e.g. on beliefs and attitudes, so we resort to interrogation. Interrogation is one method of finding out why a person thinks, behaves or believes in a particular way. Interrogation, using interviews and questionnaires on an appropriate population, is also used to confirm hypotheses. Such an hypothesis as 'most people would prefer to have a job that is a challenge rather than one which is undemanding' may be tested by field survey.

Interrogation is still the main method used in social research, including market research, as the data frequently refers to mental states which often the subject alone is capable of knowing. Thus Webb *et al.* comment:

'Today, the dominant mass of social science research is based upon interviews and questionnaires. We lament this overdependence upon a single, fallible method. Interviews and questionnaires intrude as a foreign element into the social setting they would describe, they create as well as measure attitudes, they elicit atypical roles and responses, they are limited to those who are accessible and will co-operate, and the responses obtained are produced in part by dimensions of individual differences irrelevant to the topic at hand.

'But the principal objection is that they are used alone. No research method is without bias. Interviews and questionnaires must be supplemented by methods testing the same social science variables but having different methodological weaknesses.'[1]

Some of the forms of interrogation in market and social research are shown in Fig. 14.

Interviews and Postal Surveys

Each of the above has its strengths and weaknesses. The personal interview has the advantage of flexibility and the disadvantage of cost. Also on occasions, for example in most industrial marketing research, it is a slow process as it is rarely possible to substitute for absent respondents within a firm, and it may bias the sample if a completely different firm is substituted.

[1] Eugene J. Webb, Donald T. Campbell, Richard D. Schwartz and Lee Sechrest, *Unobtrusive Measures*, Rand McNally & Co., Chicago, 1966, p. 1.

The interview can be made highly structured by using an interview schedule containing a set wording and sequence of questions. Where this is combined with fixed alternative answers, the interview restricts itself to the collection of straightforward items of information, and there is a danger of forcing answers to conform with the questionnaire pattern. The unstructured interview, on the other hand, allows the interviewer to probe and to use open ended questions that give the respondent free rein over the type of answer he gives, so, perhaps, giving the analyst new ideas on avenues to explore. Open-ended questions are often combined with a 'funnel approach' to asking questions, whereby the questions become more narrowly

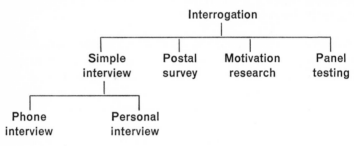

Figure 14

focused, after an initial broad question, to orient the respondent to the nature of the survey.

Telephone interviewing may have the advantage of speed in making and recording interviews, but it has the disadvantage that not everyone in a selected population may have a telephone.

The postal survey has the advantage of economy, and allows the respondent time to consult others or to refer to records. However, those replying may not be a random sample of those to whom the questionnaire was sent. There is usually a need to check on a sample of the non-respondents by personal or telephone interview. Also, it is claimed that roughly 5 per cent of those selected can be deducted for each question asked, so that, roughly, setting twenty questions will deter almost everyone from replying.

Motivation Research

Motivation research refers to the use of intensive, disguised qualitative, clinical procedures in discovering buying motives.

96

Depth interviewing is the principal technique, though it varies with interviewers. At one extreme of such interviewing is a fairly structured approach with predetermined opening questions followed by non-directive probes; at the other extreme is psychoanalytic interviewing designed to explore emotional contexts, symbolic meanings, and fantasies that may be associated with some subject. There might be interviews in groups to give respondents an opportunity to interact with others.

Motivation research also uses projective techniques. A basic assumption of these techniques is that, the more ambiguous the stimulus, the greater the scope which the situation offers for the respondent to project into his answers his motivations and values. They are of the following types:

1. Association techniques, e.g. word association tests, where the subject is presented with a word and asked to say immediately what it brings to mind.
2. Construction techniques, e.g. picture interpretations, where the subject constructs a story about the picture.
3. Completion techniques, e.g. sentence completion, where the subject is asked to complete a sentence at high speed.
4. Expressive techniques, e.g. play therapy where the emphasis is on the way the subject expresses his emotions and sentiments as he plays.

Perhaps the name 'motivation research' is a little misleading, since the approach does not lead to sampling for population parameters but for ideas. The samples taken are usually neither representative nor random. The emotional associations investigated are highly personal, while the psychoanalytic interpretations often suggested are tested neither for validity nor reliability.

Panels

Panels are used extensively in consumer market research, but not in industrial marketing where buying influences are more diffuse, the population is small and executives are neither willing nor permitted to devote their time to panel work. There is also some difficulty in obtaining continuity of membership and the danger of members becoming no longer representative of the population from which they were drawn.

G

Difficulties in Surveys

In all surveys, there are real difficulties in getting measurable counterparts for the concepts used in the hypothesis and testing the measures for reliability and validity. There is also the initial difficulty in framing hypotheses that can be tested. For example, one hypothesis quoted in organization theory is that, as an organization grows, its structure changes to combat the forces tending to destroy it. I would suggest that all changes in organization structure initiated by management could be interpreted to support this hypothesis. In other words, as it is worded, it is doubtful whether the hypothesis can be disproved, i.e. it is a truism.

There is the possibility of bias on the part of the observed or respondent, associated with his emotional involvement in the subject matter and the possibility of his being unable or unwilling to provide or recall the answers sought.

1. The respondent may not give honest replies. For example, he may seek to give a good impression by giving socially acceptable replies. The respondent needs to be encouraged to give honest replies by using interviewers who have rapport with him and who ask questions that seem to be relevant to his interests and are couched in a language that is neutral and familiar. Certainly the anonymity of the survey may have to be stressed, while question design should not suggest that some answers are more acceptable than others (unless of course, the purpose of the interview is to discover those who are prepared to deviate from the socially acceptable).
2. If the respondent believes that the results of the inquiry will affect his interest, his replies may be biased. This is difficult to avoid, as one way of gaining his co-operation is to show at the commencement of the interview that the results of the survey are related to his interest.
3. The respondent may 'change' during the process of the inquiry. Thus a consumer panel concerned with recording prices of goods purchased may eventually cease to be a representative sample o the population since greater attention to prices may alter their behaviour.
4. Where multi-choice answers are listed, respondents show a preference for strong rather than moderate statements.

There is also the possibility of bias due to the interviewer or questionnaire.

1. The interviewer's own opinions or manner may influence replies, as may his race, sex, dress or socio-economic level.
2. Replies have been influenced by the order in which questions are given, the words used, the number of response options provided, and whether they are presented pictorially or verbally.

Finally, there is the problem of sampling bias, as only a small part of the population is conveniently accessible to interview at any one time. Webb comments as follows:

'In the earliest days of polling, people were questioned in public places, probably excluding some 80% of the total population. Shifting to in-home interviewing with quota controls and no call-backs still excluded some 60%—perhaps 5% inaccessible in homes under any conditions, 25% not at home, 25% refusals, and 5% through interviewers' reluctance to approach homes of extreme wealth or poverty and a tendency to avoid fourth floor walkups.

'Under modern probability sampling with call-backs and household designation, perhaps only 15% of the population is excluded: 5% are totally inaccessible in private residences (e.g. those institutionalized, hospitalized, homeless, transient, in the military, mentally incompetent, and so forth), another 10% refuse to answer, are unavailable after three call-backs, or have moved to no known address.'[1]

Webb argues for validity checks on survey methods and advocates, in addition to more direct observation, using the evidence of physical traces and archival records. Thus physical traces can be used for measuring the incidence of some event. He quotes that the greater wear of tiles around mobile exhibits as opposed to static ones to indicate they draw more viewers. Similarly, archival records can be a check on the accuracy of replies from respondents. For example, records on absenteeism can be correlated with morale scores.

The frequent lack of objective criteria to act as independent measures with which to compare survey data, makes it difficult to check such data for reliability. Reliance is often placed on

[1] Ibid., p. 24.

analysing the data for interval logic and consistency. In fact, of course, the absence of such measures has often led to initiating the survey. Where verbal reports match some corresponding non-verbal behaviour, this can be evidence for the validity of the survey, but honest opinions do not always have a consistent behavioural counterpart. Even attitude surveys, whether based on direct or indirect methods, are difficult to test for validity. As Selltiz, Jahoda, Deutsch and Cook point out:

> 'As we indicated earlier, many questions have been raised about the validity of indirect techniques, and relatively little research evidence is available to answer them. Actually, as noted in the preceding chapter, there is not much evidence of the validity of direct techniques depending on self-report, such as interviews and questionnaires. The validity of such instruments is less often questioned, however, probably because of the "obvious" relevance of the questions to the characteristics they are intended to measure. It is the degree of inference involved in indirect tests—the gap between the subject's response and the characteristic it is presumed to indicate—that intensifies questions about validity.'[1]

Content Analysis

One technique that would fall into Webb's category of unobtrusive measures is content analysis, which may be defined as a procedure for analysing communication and classifying its content into a number of predetermined categories as a basis for making inferences. In content analysis there is usually no direct observation of behaviour, but simply an analysis of what the subject said in one of his communications. Content analysis has a number of uses:

1. To analyse the content of communication:
    (*a*) to detect trends in the content of communication, for example, to indicate a change in attitudes of newspaper editorials;
    (*b*) to test some hypothesis, for example the persuasive force of an advertisement;
    (*c*) to determine the style or technique used to persuade, such as in enemy propaganda.
2. To gauge the intention of those making the communication.

[1] C. Selltiz, M. Jahoda, M. Deutsch and S. W. Cook, *Research Methods in Social Relations*, Methuen, London, 1962, p. 311.

As yet this is mainly a matter of guesswork, for there is no validated theory to relate the content of communication to the motives of the sender.

3. To gauge the effects of the message on its audience. There can never be a one-to-one correspondence between type of message and type of effect, as audiences and circumstances differ.

The use of content analysis is increasing in marketing (particularly in advertising) though much of it lacks a sufficiently good theoretical base to yield, in itself, highly valid results.

Once the purpose of a content analysis has been defined, the next step is to define the appropriate population from which samples of communication are to be taken. Following this, the next step in the procedure is to lay down the units of analysis.

1. The recording unit is the unit to be coded in the communication. The coder could be classifying:
   (a) the words or symbols used;
   (b) type of persons mentioned, e.g. housewife, in advertisement;
   (c) sentences (though these are not easy to classify into mutually exclusive categories);
   (d) themes. (There is difficulty in breaking down a communication into themes, e.g. breaking down some advertisement on the basis of persuasive appeals used. The problem lies in finding definitions of the categories that are sufficiently operational to provide mutually exclusive and exhaustive categories that can also be reliably coded.)
2. Sometimes the context has to be examined as an aid to classifying the recording unit. This is the unit of context. Thus, if we were analysing each interaction between two people for themes, the unit of context may on occasions extend to several interactions before the coder can correctly categorize the theme.
3. The unit of enumeration presents the findings of the analysis. It will thus depend on the nature of the research. It could differ from the recording unit, or unit of context, e.g. a theme could be the recording unit, but the interaction itself could be the unit of enumeration.

It has frequently been shown that using different recording, context, or enumeration units will affect the results of the analysis. Often, of course, the results point in the same direction, but differ in magnitude. The inferences often made from a content analysis may in themselves raise theoretical issues. Is there justification for assuming that the relative frequency with which something appears in a message is a valid measure of concern for the subject?

There are also a number of statistical problems. There is a need for a sampling plan to choose a sample from the population of interest, e.g. all advertisements for detergents. Additionally there is a need to test for reliability of coding. Sometimes it is possible to get out a dictionary that classifies every item of interest, so allowing the coder simply to check the dictionary for categorizing an item. Statistical tests for measuring reliability and determining acceptable levels of reliability have been developed.[1]

HYPOTHETICAL CONSTRUCTS AND PSYCHOLOGICAL RELATIONSHIPS

Psychologists are concerned with establishing motives and functional relationships.

Possible functional relationships are:
1. Overt behaviour response to some external stimulus: $R = F(S)$.
2. Overt behaviour response to some known neurophysiological or mental state: $R = F(N)$.
3. Some known neurological or mental state response to an external stimulus: $N = F(S)$.

A possible non-causal relationship is

4. The correlation between two overt behaviour responses, as when the performance on a test is related to the performance on a job: $R_1 = F(R_2)$.

The difficulty in establishing relationships 2 and 3 lies in the psychologist's frequent inability to measure what is happening in mind and body. This has given rise to hypothetical constructs, a term used to cover entities or subjective states whose existence is inferred as they cannot be directly observed.

Social scientists seek a measure of these constructs in behaviour. The leap from behaviour to inferred state is what has to be justified. (Of course the layman seems to have no difficulty in bridging the

---

[1] Ole R. Holsti, *Content Analysis for Social Sciences and Humanities*, Addison-Wesley Publishing Co., Reading, Mass., 1969.

gap, as he dogmatically asserts that a person is immature or lacks motivations!)

The attributes of the inferred entity have 'surplus meaning' because they go beyond what is necessary and sufficient to summarize relevant observable data associated with the entity. Thus, attitude, defined in terms of predisposition to react, is something more than expressed beliefs and opinions, though these tend to be the surrogate indicators of attitude.

Those psychologists using hypothetical constructs look for these further relationships:

5. The hypothetical state of the organism as a response to some past, present, or continuing sequence of events.
6. Overt behaviour response to some hypothetical state of the organism.
7. The relationship between two hypothetical states of the organism.

Hypothetical constructs are sometimes referred to as 'intervening variables', to stress the role they usually play in intervening between the measurable stimulus and the measurable response. However, MacCorquodale and Meehl recommend that the two terms should be distinguished and that the use of the term 'intervening variable' should be restricted to the manifest behaviour.

'Such a variable will then be simply a quantity obtained by a specified manipulation of the values of empirical variables; it will involve no hypothesis as to the existence of non-observed entities or the occurrence of unobserved processes; it will contain, in its complete statement for all purposes of theory and prediction, no words which are not definable either explicitly or by reduction sentences in terms of the empirical variables; and the validity of empirical laws involving only observables will constitute both the necessary and sufficient conditions for the validity of the laws involving these intervening variables.'[1]

They go on to argue that the term 'hypothetical construct' should be defined in the way already indicated. Certainly, a generally agreed term is needed for the identifiable behaviour (Stevens used the word 'indicant'), but whether 'intervening variable' is the most suitable depends on acknowledging that all hypothetical constructs

[1] Kenneth MacCorquodale and Paul E. Meehl, 'Hypothetical Constructs and Interviewing Variables', *Psychological Review*, **55**, 1948.

play an intervening role. An examination of 5, 6 and 7 above would suggest they may not.

Northrop distinguishes between 'concepts by intuition' which get their meaning from immediately apprehended fact, and 'concepts by postulation' which take their meaning from the theory of which they are part. Hypothetical constructs would be concepts by postulation, and thus have no meaning apart from the theory which embodies them. Blue, as a colour, is a concept by intuition, but blue as the 'number of a wavelength in electromagnetic theory' is a concept by postulation, and its meaning is derived from such theory. Northrop points out that when seemingly the same concept by postulation is used in two different theories, it is highly unlikely that it has exactly the same meaning in both. He argues that this is a constant source of confusion—this failure to recognize that the meaning of any concept by postulation is embodied in the postulates of the theoretical system of which it is part:[1]

'A concept by postulation gets its meanings from the postulates of some specific, deductively formulated theory in which it occurs. This is what it means, and this is all that it means. No reduction to commonsense objects or to sense data is necessary or required.'

Northrop also argues that concepts by postulation and concepts by intuition belong to different worlds of discourse and should not be treated in the same context. Thus it is silly to speak of electrons being noisy or pink. However, the real importance of Northrop's argument lies in its insistence that a scientific theory containing the concepts by postulation must be constructed independently of the operational definitions of these concepts.

Coombs's distinction between phenotypic and genotypic levels of description corresponds to the distinction between surrogate indicators or operational definitions and the hypothetical constructs they reflect. Description at the phenotypic level refers to the observed or manifest behaviour, e.g. the performance score on a test of subjects A and B. Description at the genotypic level refers to the level of behaviour that is inferred to underlie or generate the phenotypic level, e.g. the inference that A has more ability than B as inferred from the test scores.[2]

[1] F. S. C. Northrop, *The Logic of the Sciences and the Humanities*, Meridian Books, The World Publishing Co., New York, 1959, p. 113.
[2] Clyde H. Coombs, 'Theory and Methods of Social Measurement' in *Research*

Hypothetical constructs have a systematic as opposed to real existence, as they are entities that play a part in some system which may or may not have an exact counterpart in reality. What then is the status of such concepts, since the only denotation they have is that provided by the observables said to represent some of the components of the constructs? Obviously, if what is available through observation is all that is needed for understanding, prediction and control, then the introduction of hypothetical constructs is superfluous. In fact their introduction can be confusing, as psychologists may within the same context treat such concept (e.g. attitude, morale, intelligence) as hypothetical constructs, and then deal with their measurable counterpart without emphasizing the distinction. Also, differences in the measurement of an hypothetical construct by independent researchers, may have different results, leading perhaps wrongly to the conclusion that these were contradictory, whereas the experiments were not dealing with the same phenomena.

One fundamental tenet of behaviourism in its early days was a refusal to admit any inferred subjective states, such as motives, in psychological research. Only observable data were acceptable as evidence. Early behaviourism can be regarded as a 'thoroughgoing operational analysis of traditional mental concepts' that went too far. Bridgman, the physicist, similarly argued that things which could not be directly observed and measured had no physical existence. They were simply products of the imagination—invented and not discovered—though they might be useful in visualizing a process. To Bridgman, terms should summarize classes of observed fact and not contain attributes that go beyond observations. In other words, for Bridgman, hypothetical constructs gave rise to the fallacy of reification.

Bertrand Russell also argued that, wherever possible, hypothetical constructs should be avoided. He said that they arose because the manifestation of some hypothetical construct was not equivalent to the construct itself, so it came to be regarded as distinct from any of its manifestations. (This is the 'surplus meaning' concept already discussed.) However, he believed that 'economy demands that we should identify the thing with the class of its appearances'. Recognizing that the opposite of belief in the real existence of hypothetical constructs is not disbelief (as this is a form of belief

Methods in the Behavioural Sciences, ed. Leon Festinger and Daniel Katz, Holt, Rinehart & Winston, New York, 1966, ch. 11, p. 471.

itself) but doubt, he advocated that the researcher should not assert the existence of such unnecessary entities.

It is true that some social scientists have argued that the failure of an observable counterpart to indicate the existence of an hypothetical construct cannot be used to deny its reality. Thus the fact that our attempts to measure I.Q. with the precision required for our purposes have not met with success, does not mean there is no such entity. One-to-one correspondence between the hypothetical construct (say, the abstract idea of attitude) and the operational definition (say, consisting of verbal reports of attitude) is impossible.

Russell would perhaps agree with this, but argue that the onus still rests on those who develop the hypothetical construct to find evidence for its existence. But is it necessary to prove the existence of an hypothetical construct? The arguments so far would suggest that it is better simply to regard hypothetical constructs as having systematic existence, so that we test not so much for their existence, as for their utility within the system.

Most psychologists would perhaps now admit that some mental event occurs between the stimulus and the overt response, which can radically affect the way the stimulus is perceived, and hence the nature of the subject's response. Even in science the subject never sees the ultimate components of matter, but infers their behaviour and properties to explain and co-ordinate his experiments. Hypothetical constructs help in the search for hypotheses. When a concept is confined to observable data, there is no 'surplus meaning' to use as a basis for developing predictive hypotheses.

Creativity manifests itself in developing hypothetical constructs, rich in meaning and potential for developing ideas to be tested. As Northrop says,

'. . . a science which restricts itself to directly observable entities and relations automatically loses predictive power. The science tends, even when deductively formulated, to be merely descriptive and to accomplish little more so far as prediction is concerned than to express the hope that the sensed relations holding between the entities of one's subject matter today will recur tomorrow.'[1]

Even Russell, in a sense, admits that the hypothetical construct will form the basis for empirical research. He suggests making statements containing hypothetical constructs more realistic:

[1] Northrop, op. cit., p. 115.

'Given a set of propositions nominally dealing with supposed inferred entities, we observe the properties which are required of the supposed entities in order to make these propositions true. By dint of a little logical ingenuity, we then construct some logical function of less hypothetical entities which has the requisite properties. This constructed function we substitute for the supposed inferred entities, and thereby obtain a new and less doubtful interpretation of the body of propositions in question.'[1]

The difficulty of dealing with antecedents (stimuli) and consequences (responses) has facilitated the acceptance of hypothetical constructs by psychologists. Thus, if a psychologist ignores the hypothetical constructs that act as mediators then, as an example, for eight distinct antecedents and ten distinct consequents, he would have to deal with possibly $8 \times 10 = 80$ relationships. However, when each antecedent is related to a mediator which is related to one consequent, the number of relationships would be $8 + 10 = 18$.

The validation of hypothetical constructs is a difficult problem. Northrop distinguishes epistemic correlation from statistical correlation. He uses the term 'epistemic correlation' to denote the relation between the hypothetical construct and its operational definition in terms of some observable counterpart. In contrast, he argues that statistical correlation relates items that are in the same world of discourse. He states that validating hypothetical constructs will necessitate establishing the appropriate epistemic correlations. Hence, without operational definitions there can be no validation.

Validation of a construct can take a number of forms, but all depend on having some operational measure of the construct. Thus we may argue that if a construct is valid, its operational measure should lead to predictions that can be confirmed. For example, the prediction that two groups known to differ can be distinguished on the basis of some operational measure of the construct assumed to account for their difference. Alternatively, measures of the same construct should correlate or each element in the hypothetical construct should correlate in the way predicted by the theory.

Turner, after arguing that hypothetical constructs can be described

[1] Bertrand Russell, 'The Relation of Sense-Data to Physics' in *Philosophy of Science*, ed. Arthur Danto and Sydney Morgenbesser, Meridian Books, The World Publishing Co., New York, p. 42.

as being 'as if' constructs because it is 'as if' some hypothetical construct lies behind the data we observe, points out that

'. . . One cannot say that a theoretical construct is definitely true, for alternative constructions of theoretical entities may serve just as well to suggest the events. And it may be that no experiment can decide the issue among alternatives.'[1]

[1] M. B. Turner, *Philosophy and the Science of Behaviour*, Appleton-Century-Crofts Inc., New York, 1967, p. 172.

Chapter 6

STATISTICAL GENERALIZATION AND MEASUREMENT

STATISTICAL GENERALIZATION

Statistical generalization is a term usually reserved for the discovery of:

1. Regularities between attributes or variables; a variable being defined as something measurable that can assume different magnitudes, and an attribute as anything whose presence or absence can be noted without any measurement. For example, one statistical regularity between variables would be between I.Q. and test scores, while between attributes it could be the percentage of people in the population having personality X, and the percentage of consumers with personality X buying brand Y. However, an attribute is really a special case of the variable: it is a binary variable.

2. The fraction of instances or the probability of an event occurring, given some particular situation: this form of statistical generalization could be some generalization about a population on the basis of samples drawn from it; or about a sample from knowledge of the population; or about future samples on the basis of one sample already drawn.

The statistical generalization in itself does not constitute an explanation, but can suggest one. The 'why' remains to be answered. Thus it may be noted that women over 45 and under 65 are more innovative with new products than women of other age groups. This is not an explanation, but may direct research and suggest explanations, e.g. that women within this age group have more time on their hands. Of course, as we have seen, the hypothesis often comes first and the statistical generalization is sought merely as confirmation. Theory may suggest the consequence that 'workers are less likely to strike over a principle than over a claim for higher wages'. Such a consequence as a generalization can be checked by statistical sampling.

109

Arguments from statistical generalizations can only be probable. Thus:

1. Most individuals under circumstances C are people who behave in manner A.
2. X on occasion T was in circumstances C.
3. Therefore probably the individual X on occasion T is a person who behaved in manner A.

The theory of probability is concerned with estimating the rational expectation of an occurrence as against its non-occurrence. But many generalizations are not based on statistical sampling, but on the selection of instances, which are quoted as proof of a tendency. Opposing instances are explained away as simply reflecting unusual circumstances. Later the tendency is treated as a universal law, so that a mathematical superstructure can be erected, and the subject degenerates into mere exercises in deduction of little practical import.

We are all obliged to make generalizations on the basis of our experience without the benefit of having them tested by formal statistical sampling. The important point is to recognize the limited basis of our belief. We would all prefer to say that 'all X tend to be Y' because it is more precise than 'some X is Y', but to do so suggests that we have evidence of a scientific nature.

As Morris Cohen pointed out, social science is bedevilled by disputes arising from belief in tendencies not based on adequate sampling. Thus one group argues that people seek consistency between beliefs themselves and between their beliefs and their behaviour. Explanations and elaborate reasoning are based on this premise. Others argue that, on the contrary, people tend to ignore or gloss over such inconsistencies by examining their beliefs singly and not collectively, while there is also a tendency for what people say and what they do to differ. There is truth in both statements but only statistical investigation or validated theory can decide in which circumstances either one will predominate.

PROBABILITY

1. Subjective probability is the psychological interpretation of probability, and measures the confidence a person has in something being true. No justification is offered for the belief. Such

probabilities can differ from person to person, and are often unstable for even the same person. It can be defined operationally as the odds a person would accept if betting on its truth. Thus, if a person would lay 8 to 2 on its truth, then his subjective estimate of probability is 0·8 (8/10). Whether such betting odds do in fact measure actual degrees of credibility is a matter of controversy.

The advantage of subjective probabilities is that they can be used in advance of observation. Although labelled 'subjective' because they represent individual opinion, they are objective in the sense that they can be publicly tested.

2. Deductive or *a priori* probability is a logical interpretation of probability. Laplace in the eighteenth century defined it as the ratio of the number of favourable cases relating to an event to the total number of equally possible events. For example, because a coin is equally likely to come up heads or tails, the probability of a head is 0·5. The problem here is ensuring that events are equally possible, e.g. that the coin is indeed unbiased. The essential principle, embodied in Laplace's 'Principle of Non-Sufficient Reason' or Keynes's 'Principle of Indifference', is the assertion that *a priori* probability is appropriate if there is no reason to deny that some set of indivisible events are all equally possible.

3. The relative frequency interpretation of probability establishes probability empirically. Here the probability of X occurring is the relative frequency with which X does occur in the situation being discussed. Thus, if 1,000 tosses of a coin result in 529 heads, the estimate of probability of a heads is $529/1000 = 0·529$.

The probability could be just based on history, as when we establish the probability of male births to female births from an examination of past census data. As probability differs here with sample size, Von Mises argues that probability should be determined by taking the limit of relative frequency—that is, the relative frequency that changes negligibly as sample size increases.

Probability based on relative frequency is more acceptable when based on some theory, as in Mendel's laws on heredity. Unfortunately, such laws are seldom available in social science, so that we have to rely on historical records or on a limited number of trials.

In assessing a statistical generalization, the first question is whether

111

the correct population was selected for the purpose at hand. One company for six years conducted market surveys among men only, about sock purchases. In fact, fifty per cent of all men's socks were purchased by women, though women were not interviewed; thus the results of the survey were not representative of the population of sock-buyers. On the other hand, a company may survey the nominal buyers of a product, when such buyers are in reality merely agents acting on behalf of someone else. Such samplings of the wrong population stem perhaps more from errors in problem definition than from any lack of statistical sophistication. A sample needs to be representative, and the method by which the sub-set is to be taken is the sample design. This is inferred if a sample is drawn in a manner that ensures the randomness or some other procedure that guards against bias.

In general, these rules apply:

1. The larger the random sample, the more accurate will be the estimate of the population parameter.
2. Stratified sampling is likely to produce more accurate samples if the population is heterogeneous, as this ensures that different elements in the population are represented. In stratified sampling the population is divided into homogeneous groups or strata to which are allocated specific portions of the total sample.
3. The wider the margin of error that is allowed, the more accurate can be the estimate within that margin of error.

The danger in all statistical generalization is that population characteristics may be changing, so that samples drawn today may not be predictive of future populations. This lack of population stability can undermine market research. Products designed to specifications based on market research may be unacceptable, not because market research failed to tap real opinions at the time, but because these have changed in the interval between the market survey and the market test.

MEASUREMENT

In certain cases relationships, whether causal or otherwise, can be expressed in a quantitative form. Such measurement helps in the making of comparisons and allows finer discriminations to be made. Both explanation and description can be made more precise

112

by the addition of measurements to the statements. Mathematics is essential for establishing with precision the general structural relationships within some system. Also, if the system is represented by symbols, structural relationships can be highlighted to facilitate understanding.

In a sense we are all obliged to do mathematics, but do so without the efficiency of using mathematical method with its symbolism, rich collection of techniques, and proofs, that save time and allow generalization.

There is no question of mathematics merely providing a more concise and elegant language for what can be discovered by non-mathematical means. Many results in the physical sciences emanate directly from mathematics; they can be expressed only mathematically, and often the original hypothesis can be conceived only by a mathematician.

Coombs, in his 'Theory of Data', sets out a classification system that allows different types of psychological data to be related to the various models available to analyse such data.

'It is probably generally true that a method for analysing data implies certain conditions that must be met by the method of collecting the data but there are many variations in the methods of collecting data that may satisfy the same conditions. When these conditions become clear the full generality of the methods for analysing data becomes apparent. This generality is obscured by terminology particular to a context as in psychophysics or attitude-scaling and it would seem desirable to abstract the properties of all methods and see thereby what is common among them and how they differ.

'The theory of data proposes to do this. It proposes to provide a foundation for models of psychological measurement and classify, systematize, and interrelate them.'[1]

In physical science, mathematical relationships can be established to allow extrapolation for coping with the problem of size. However, with regard to human behaviour there may be no logical relationship between an individual's behaviour in a dyad and in a group of (say) five; even if there is some logical relationship, it is doubtful whether it would follow the deductive pattern required by

---

[1] Clyde H. Coombs, 'A Theory of Data', *The Psychological Review*, **67**, May 1960.

mathematical formulations. In fact, the absence generally of relationships that follow a mathematical logic between micro- and macro-behaviour impedes the practical application of mathematics to social phenomena.

There are other difficulties. For example, consumer responses to promotional effort are apt to be highly non-linear, and some minimum level of promotion is necessary before any response can even be detected. There is also the problem of carry-over from one period to another. Further problems lie in getting out operational measures of hypothetical constructs and gauging the interaction effects when there are many variables to consider. Add to all this the pressure of time, and we understand why mathematical models are seldom used in day-to-day marketing.

An obsession with measurement can divert attention from more substantive issues. Thus, the attention given to attitude measurement between the wars led to an ignoring of the more substantive problem of attitude change. There can be premature quantification, in that the mathematical superstructure lacks an adequate conceptual base; no amount of mathematical manipulation will make up for the poverty of an underlying conceptual structure. The conceptual base must come first, and this is likely in social science to be composed largely of qualitative judgments. Premature emphasis on mathematics is difficult to avoid, since only the quantitative is often judged of value and researchers often feel too uncertain of themselves not to be seduced by Lord Kelvin's dictum.[1]

The role of mathematics and statistics is increasing. In spite of what has been said, the area of application is very wide. Even in the sphere of classification they play a part. Thus it may not be possible to determine the classification of an item on the basis of just one dimension, but only on the basis of several dimensions examined collectively. Discriminant analysis is a statistical technique for doing this. Similarly, when a set of data is classified on two different bases (e.g. accidents as they actually occur throughout the working day and as they would occur if spread evenly over the working day), the χ^2 ('chi-square') test can be used to check whether the difference between them is explicable by chance.

All measurement procedures should be tested for reliability and validity. One operational measure of reliability focuses on

[1] A remark attributed to Lord Kelvin was that 'unless a thing can be measured quantitatively, it does not exist significantly'.

consistency in results. High reliability entails high agreement between the results of measuring the same thing twice or in different ways. For example, where there is no agreement between measurement of people's attitudes from one day to the next then either the measurement is unreliable or the quality being measured is not stable. Where the variance stems from defects in the measurement instrument, it is composed of systematic bias and random error. Thus high reliability suggests only that results can be reproduced within certain chance limits.

Construct validity is concerned with whether the measure measures what it sets out to measure. On the other hand, predictive validity is often tested by showing the predictive power of the measurement, or the high correlation between measures and criterion. Thus the validity of aptitude tests are demonstrated by showing that scores on the tests are highly correlated to success on jobs requiring such aptitudes.

Construct and predictive validity are the main types, but there are others which will be discussed later. Construct validity is fundamental, since it is also concerned with validating the theory itself as a consequence of validating its constructs. In recent years it has made increasing use of factor analysis.

The capacity to translate qualities into quantitative terms is the aim in all scientific inquiry. However, progress in measurement has meant abandoning the view that the measurement of a quality can always be represented by a single number or scalar, as in classical mathematics. As in the measurement of density and force, several numbers (or vectors) may be required.

When we produce operational measures of hypothetical constructs, we need to devise a method for assigning numbers to represent the observations we make. The problem is to produce a method or rule of correspondence for mapping or assigning members of one set (e.g. responses to questions) into members of another set (e.g. numerical scale) to reflect degree of belief. Where there is a valid rule of correspondence, the two sets are isomorphic to each other for the purpose at hand.

Nominal, Ordinal, Interval and Ratio Scales

The nature of the data sets a limit to the mathematical operations that are legitimate. We may only be able to count the numbers in each category; thus each category is the same number, but different categories have different numbers. Such categorizing and numbering is known as nominal measurement. Apart from the nominal scale, where numbers are merely used as labels to identify, a number of other measurement scales can be distinguished.

The term 'scaling' rather than 'measuring' is sometimes used for the ordinal scale where items are ranked in series or grouped into classes according to the degree of the quality possessed. In an ordinal scale the relationship between the items is asymmetrical, that is, if A is more emotional than B, B is not more emotional than A. The relationship is also transitive: if A is more emotional than B, and B is more emotional than C, then A is more emotional than C. A transitive relationship may be difficult to achieve, because the constructs involved are multidimensional. Kerlinger quotes the construct 'dominate' as an example: 'A wife may dominate her husband and the husband may dominate the child, but the child may dominate the mother (the wife).'[1] Even consumer preferences are not always transitive. A may be preferred to B, and B to C, but C may be preferred to A. Establishing such triads can be used to measure the internal consistency of a scale. On an ordinal scale there is no indication of distances between items in the series; the numbers simply indicate rank order. Items in an ordinal scale can be correlated to other ranked series, and medians can be calculated, but addition, subtraction, multiplication and division are not possible, for example, it is not legitimate to add up distances within a scale.

In an interval scale, equal intervals on the scale represent equal amounts of change, e.g. temperature scale. Thus going from 100 to 110 involves the same change as going from 120 to 130. There is no absolute zero point that has been empirically established, so that multiplication and division are not possible, though the calculation of the mean and standard deviation are.

Thus the true zero point might be 100 points below that currently used, so that the two intervals quoted above become 200 to 210 and 220 to 230. As the interval is still 10 for each, this allows us to add or subtract intervals and to calculate a mean and standard deviation. But to multiply and divide would be wrong; for example, from 100 to 110 is a rise of 10%, but if the zero point is arbitrary and the true change is from 200 to 210, then the rise is only 5%.

A ratio or cardinal scale has the properties of the interval scale,

[1] F. N. Kerlinger, *Foundations of Behavioral Research*, Holt, Rinehart & Winston, New York, 1964, p. 421.

but because it has a natural absolute zero base, multiplication and division are possible. Many statistical techniques only appropriate to interval or ratio scales are applied to social science data where there is often doubt as to whether such data conforms to these scales.

Chapter 7

TELEOLOGICAL AND GENETIC EXPLANATIONS

TELEOLOGICAL EXPLANATIONS

A teleological or teleonomic explanation does not explain in terms of origins or causes, but in terms of either the goals being sought or the function some component performs in a system. However, Kurtz and others have argued that in essence teleological explanations are still essentially causal explanations, the differences resulting from modes of expression and form rather than substance.

Motives

The first type of teleological explanation is in the nature of an hypothesis as to motives. Every businessman sometimes speculates on why someone behaved as he did. People—whether customers, managers, subordinates or peers—may not give their real reasons for opposition to some proposal. Reasons may have to be discovered.

On the surface it appears with motives that goals cause present behaviour; that future events direct current actions; or 'that goals or ends of activity are dynamic agents in their own realization'. It is less misleading to view present behaviour as being caused by a desire to achieve a particular goal: current expectations of achieving this results in the present forward-looking behaviour. For example, 'ambition causes a person to work hard'. This is regarded as an acceptable form of explanation in that it stems from knowledge additional to that gained from studying the behaviour itself. (However, this is not to suggest that all motives give rise to behaviour that is directed at some external goal.)

What is referred to as 'cause' is the 'motive for doing', in the sense that without some motive there would be no reason for exhibiting the pattern of behaviour under discussion. Motives constitute some of the antecedent conditions which account for subsequent behaviour. Such teleological explanations assume the presence of a conscious agent, and are common in history and psychology, where the aim is to discover reasons for doing rather than mechanical causes. Yet the establishment of motives does not establish fact. It is also an error to assume that people are always motivated by just one thing, such as to self-actualize, to be accepted by colleagues, etc. Another error is to assume that motivations are the same for every cultural group so that findings for one group can be generalized to another without testing.

Purposeful behaviour has been attributed to purely physical systems, in that machines are designed to fulfil certain functions and have components that play specific roles within the overall function. Nagel comments:

'In an age in which servo-mechanisms no longer excite wonder, and in which the language of cybernetics and "negative feed-backs" has become widely fashionable, the imputation of "goal-directed" behaviour to purely physical systems certainly cannot be rejected as an absurdity. Whether "purposes" can also be imputed to such physical systems, as some expounders of cyber-netics claim, is perhaps doubtful . . . .'

Kurtz points out that the term 'motives' may be used in the sense of 'justifying reasons', with no scientific explanation nor validation of either the particular motive construct quoted or its general relationship with consequent behaviour.[2] Yet there is often a need to know underlying motives. Like the historian, the manager may wish to understand past events in terms of explaining people's behaviour. On occasions a manager may suspect that reasons put forward disguise real motives. He must find the real reasons if he is to devise a strategy that meets the real needs of the situation.

The problem then lies in discovering motives. The limitations of motivation research have already been discussed. In any case, it is not a technique for day-to-day use. The various theories of motivation are at too high a level of generality to offer much guidance. In fact, in areas such as consumer buying behaviour the writers hardly bother to mention them. As Kurtz points out, motives are general or dispositional, while for predictive purposes we need to explain intention, which is a much more specific state. This

---

[1] Ernest Nagel, 'Teleological Explanation and Teleological Systems' in *Readings in the Philosophy of Science*, ed. Herbert Fiegl and May Brodbeck, Appleton-Century-Crofts Inc., New York, 1953.

[2] Paul Kurtz, *Decision and the Condition of Man*, Dell Publishing Co., New York, 1965, p. 31.

requires knowledge, not just of general dispositional factors, but of the particular circumstances operating at the time.

A's perception of *B* often influences the type of specific motives and intentions *A* attributes to *B*. This is facilitated when, as often occurs, the available evidence is consistent with contradictory hypotheses on motives. Any action can be attributed to base motives or evil intent, but the same behaviour interpreted differently will usually also support the hypothesis of innocent intent. Even where it is known that certain motives are generally influential, it does not establish that they predominate on some specific occasion.

In seeking motives and intent, do we want (as some historians claim they do) to re-experience and re-enact someone else's thought processes in the light of what we know about him and the circumstances? It can at least be a basis for creating an hypothesis, but offers no certainty. Other kinds of evidence are required, such as how past and present behaviour confirm the hypothesis. In this area, particularly, we must consider rival hypotheses in order to rule out merely collecting evidence favourable to our initial predisposition.

Unfortunately, the identification of motives can only be tentative, since the same means (behaviour) may serve many different goals, and people themselves may not be consistent in their aims. Observing a person's behaviour helps us to gauge his motives if his goals are known, or to gauge his goals if we know his motives; but behaviour cannot usually point to both goals and motives.

Functionalism

The second type of teleological explanation is referred to as functionalism, though this term is sometimes used for teleological explanations in general. A functional explanation refers to the contribution or function that some unit, act, feature or component plays in maintaining or realizing some goal of the system to which it belongs. A distinction is sometimes made between latent and manifest functions. A latent function is hidden and has unintended consequences that were intended for the function. There remains the problem of determining whether a consequence is intended or not: i.e. making the concepts operational.

In a functional explanation, interest is centred on how the system attains its ends, alters or maintains its structure through the contributions made by its components. Thus, the circulation process in the human body contributes to the goal of maintaining life by distributing food, oxygen and heat and removing waste matter from the body. It is the properties of the components of a system and their interrelationships which determine the state of a system, and this state, in turn, determines the extent to which its overall goals are achieved.

The concept of 'holism', of current interest in organization theory, asserts that the significance of a component stems from its relationship to the rest of the system, and the component itself is changed through interaction with other components. It focuses attention on functional structure, which refers to the way parts behave and change during interaction, rather than with formal structure, which simply refers to the way parts are put together.

Kurtz describes the logical form of the functional explanation thus:

> 'Functional explanations may be seen to take on the following logical form. "Given any (organic) system S (such as the liver), let us suppose p (such as the storing of glycogen) to be a property of that system. p is not always present and has values from A_0 to A_x. In order for p to be present, then, certain conditions must be present within either the system or the field, including the environment E. p and its values A_0 and A_x are a function of other conditions that must be present; let us call them r, s, t. And r, s, t themselves are within the system or its range and are also functions of p, such that variations in p cause variations in r, s, t and internal and external compensations." '[1]

He also points out that the functions performed by some component can be regarded as necessary or sufficient conditions for the emergence of certain properties of the system. Ideally, a functional explanation accounts for the occurrence of the property of some component, as well as showing the role that it plays in maintaining or changing the state or structure of the system of which it is part. Thus a true functional approach to the business as a system would first select appropriate components or sub-systems (say, decision areas), then show how the characteristics of these components (say, the way decisions are made) bring about some state of the system.

Nagel argues also that functional explanations can be expressed

[1] Ibid., p. 58.

in terms of sufficient, necessary and contributory conditions, to bring them in line with the way scientific propositions are generally expressed; a functional explanation says B is an effect of A instead of saying A is a cause or condition of B. Nagel doubts whether the translation of a teleological proposition into non-teleological terms is an equivalance, since the latter does not involve the implication of system.

Functional explanations presuppose some system within which the component plays a part and produces some effects. A system is a set of interdependent and/or interacting parts which together perform some function. As any system can be shown to be a sub-system of some larger system (just as a carburettor system can be shown to be a sub-system of the car engine), the appropriate boundaries of a system are determined by the goals sought. However, even when there is agreement on goals, there may still be debate over system. A systems and procedures specialist argues that he needs to look at the total interdepartmental network of procedures; that to examine any smaller system might lead to sub-optimization. Top management, although agreeing with the efficiency goal, argues that cost and time considerations rule out an investigation of such a total network.

'This debate over system is not merely academic. To study too wide a system for the purpose at hand is wasteful, but to study too narrow a system may lead to sectional efficiency at the expense of the total system. If a particular system seeks to achieve certain objectives at minimum cost, it is not likely to do so by seeking separately to minimize cost for each of the sub-systems, since overall minimum cost may necessitate high cost in one sub-system to achieve low cost elsewhere. For instance, a motor manufacturer might reduce the cost of piston rings by increasing their production and consequently spreading the fixed costs: but unless he can simultaneously make more pistons and cylinder blocks he will only increase the overall cost by accumulating an expensive surplus. It is the interdependence of sub-systems from the point of view of the purpose at hand that necessitates the overall approach.

'The purpose of an analysis also determines which sub-systems are appropriate. If we wish to understand how a watch works, it is of little value to study how the gold parts are arranged in relation to the brass parts if they are purely ornamental. In studying a watch as a mechanism, aesthetic aspects are irrelevant. However, in any study of the watch as a marketable commodity the system would include the watch's appearance as one important sub-system.'[1]

The concept of system is widespread in management as well as in logic and the physical and social sciences. Yet it is doubtful whether there is a theory of systems so much as a set of concepts about them. Thus a contrast is made between *static* and *dynamic* systems. A static system does not change its attributes over time; a dynamic one does. An *open* system exchanges materials, energy or information with its environment; a *closed* system does not. The environment is that part of the world outside the system which affects it by a change in its attributes. An *adaptive* system can react to its environment in a way that is favourable to its continued operation. A *stable* system is stable with respect to certain of its variables, if these fluctuate only within definable and acceptable limits. Finally, a *state-determined* system is one whose future can be determined from its initial state.

In social science there can be difficulty in defining the appropriate system of which some component is part and also in forming operational criteria to indicate the various states of the system produced by the properties of its components. Unless such states can be defined, it becomes impossible to show empirically the exact contribution of some component. Thus one social psychologist speaks of factors in a business organization that are dysfunctional to a healthy personality. The problem is to define operationally what exactly is a healthy personality. Nagel quotes Talcott Parsons:

> A sufficient proportion of people within the firm must be adequately motivated to act in accordance with the objectives of the firm though it is difficult to define people's needs or the fraction that must be satisfied.[2]

Nagel points out that it is difficult to say whether a given system satisfies prerequisites formulated in such vague and indefinite terms. There is a danger in functional explanations of assuming that the

[1] John O'Shaughnessy, *Business Organization*, Allen & Unwin, London, 1966, p. 126.
[2] Ernest Nagel, *The Structure of Science*, Routledge & Kegan Paul, London, 1961, paraphrase from p. 531.

contribution made by a component within some system can be achieved by that component only. Thus it has been argued that a loosely structured organization is to be recommended if creativity, participation and innovation are to be encouraged. Yet it can still be argued that such benefits could be achieved by some other means without incurring the possibly unpleasant side-effects of a loosely structured organization.

Nagel has also pointed out that, although knowledge of the structure of some system may be a prerequisite to a full understanding of it, this is not sufficient; laws on how the parts are dynamically interrelated are also necessary. He points out that there is no unique structure corresponding to some designated function, though a function sets limits to the number of structures that are suitable.

These views of Nagel have significance to students of organization. Knowledge of the static organization structure of a business does not allow an understanding of how the organization structure works in practice. As Kurtz points out, 'a pickled frog is not the same as a jumping frog'. There is a need to know the 'laws' lying behind the working of the organization, the stable pattern of relationships or the rules governing the interaction between the elements in the system. This point has been made by social scientists in their criticism of classical organization theory. It would appear that the search for the unique and ideal organization structure to suit a set of strategies, is in vain, as there is no one structure that gives a unique fit to a strategy.

The concept of 'function' is distinguished from that of the word 'effect' by its close association with the concept of system, purpose and contribution to goals. But functional explanations (common in sociological literature) have been subject to severe criticism particularly when the word 'function' seems to suggest a conscious directing agent.

1. Such explanations did a great deal to impede progress in science, e.g. 'polar bears are white to deceive their enemies'. A great number of such functional explanations have given way to non-teleological ones, e.g. evolution and random mutation theory explain the polar bear's whiteness. This seems more of a failure to recognize when teleological explanations are appropriate than a condemnation of teleological explanations *per se*.

2. There is doubt as to whether functional explanations are ever satisfactory, since they do not appear susceptible to forming a systematic body of laws.
3. Psychologists who adhere to the stimulus/response model tend to see man as a mechanism responding to stimuli, and reject functional explanations.

Thus Homans rejects such explanations as being in practice inadequate. He quotes social inequality as an example:

'Social inequality is thus an unconsciously evolved device by which societies ensure that the most important positions are conscientiously filled by the most qualified persons.'[1]

He claims that this statement is a 'good example of the lengths to which functionalism will lead otherwise intelligent men'.

Perhaps the final comment on functional explanations can be left to Kurtz:

'All that teleonomy involves is recognition of organization, functional parts, self-maintenance, growth and striving, not some mysterious future magnet directing the present.'[2]

GENETIC EXPLANATIONS

Hitherto we have been concerned with explanations that involve only the consideration of occurrences immediately prior to the occasion to be explained. However, there are situations that develop over a long period of time where the current unsatisfactory state has evolved through a whole series of past occurrences. The manager may wish to show the underlying origins of the present position to guide him in choosing corrective action. Alternatively, such an approach may be the best way of understanding some current situation. Thus, some complicated wage structures seem to make no sense unless we trace their history, and labour relations generally are perhaps best viewed thus.

A genetic explanation seeks to show how an existing complex problem has evolved. It is essentially an historical approach, setting out the sequence of events leading to the present position. It is an

---

[1] George C. Homans, *The Nature of Social Science*, An Original Harbinger Book, Harcourt, Brace & World Inc., New York, p. 66.
[2] Paul Kurtz, op. cit., p. 64.

ex post facto approach, in that we start with an existing problematic situation and analyse retrospectively to discover the causal chain. As a consequence, there is the ever-present danger of committing the fallacy of *post hoc, ergo propter hoc*—of confusing cause with non-causal antecedent. Although knowing the origins of a problem can be an aid to understanding them, the history of a subject is not a substitute for an analysis of the present system or situation itself if this is what is wanted. Thus, to study how some organization has evolved may not displace the need to study how the evolved organization is currently working.

Explaining 'how-possibly' some event happened by tracing the steps leading to its occurrence, is regarded by some historians as the essential historical problem. Certainly, 'colligation' has been a term used by historians to describe the explanation of an event by tracing its relationship to other events through time to form a 'significant narrative'. It is not just a matter of discovering motives or isolating contributory, necessary and sufficient conditions, but also of showing how such past conditions interconnect to form a pattern of explanation that accounts for the current state of affairs. There is no closed-system, laboratory-type experiment here, but a long chain of events which need to be woven into an explanatory pattern. It is essentially an amalgam of the forms of explanation already discovered.

The genetic explanation involves firstly listing the factors at work which have had a major influence in bringing about the current state of affairs. The history of these forces is traced out to show how one event led to another, culminating in the present situation. The criterion for choosing an event as part of the sequence is its appearance as an indispensable condition for subsequent events in the series. There is still the problem of eliminating alternative accounts of events.

Suppose, for example, we wish to explain a loss in sales and company profit. We are aware of labour disputes following the sale of the company by its owner, Smith, to a syndicate which subsequently appointed a general manager named Jones. We would like to trace the connection, if any, between these events and the drop in sales and profit. We first list the factors at work. In this case these factors are the groups of people involved, namely management, labour, and customers which 'experience' suggests were possibly instrumental in bringing about the current problematic situation.

At some point in the past at time T, the arrangement of these factors reflected an acceptable trend. At the current time C, the arrangement is unsatisfactory. The genetic explanation aims at uncovering the sequence of contributory and necessary conditions that brought about this change during the time interval T to C. This requires that the relevant history of each factor from time T to C is recorded and interactions between factors shown. Such a history can be sketched in chart form, as in Fig. 15. The statements at the side of the events on the chart take the form of factual descriptions, judgments and inferences. Thus the probable truth of a genetic explanation rests on the value of these statements whose likelihood of being true may have to be established by methods already discussed.

The genetic approach to a problem can be used to tease some pattern, model or trend out of a sequence of events. It is of course better to avoid giving emotional labels to different parts of the pattern, e.g. 'this point marks the development of labour intransigence'.

The network or pattern of events should form a coherent whole, so that no event is treated as an isolated occurrence but as an antecedent or consequent in a chain of determining events. In this way, each piece of evidence receives support from the evidence supporting the total pattern.

A genetic explanation is usually specific. It does not aim at developing explanations for kinds of events. This does not mean that genetic explanations do not assume law-like statements of a social and behavioural character. Generalizations and assumptions are inevitable as bases for interpreting and inter-relating the otherwise isolated occurrences. It is hoped to draw these generalizations from the social sciences rather than from current 'conventional wisdom', providing the decision-maker recognizes that specific circumstances may invalidate the applicability of the generalization.

GENETIC EXPLANATION

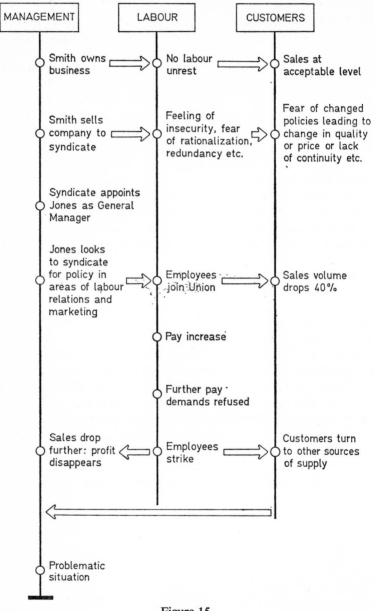

MANAGEMENT	LABOUR	CUSTOMERS
Smith owns business	No labour unrest	Sales at acceptable level
Smith sells company to syndicate	Feeling of insecurity, fear of rationalization, redundancy etc.	Fear of changed policies leading to change in quality or price or lack of continuity etc.
Syndicate appoints Jones as General Manager		
Jones looks to syndicate for policy in areas of labour relations and marketing	Employees join Union	Sales volume drops 40%
	Pay increase	
	Further pay demands refused	
Sales drop further: profit disappears	Employees strike	Customers turn to other sources of supply
Problematic situation		

Figure 15

Chapter 8

MODELS AND THEORIES

MODELS AND ISOMORPHISM

Where the pattern of relationships among the elements in a system X is identical to those in system Y, the two systems are isomorphs of each other. Thus elements A, B, C in system X have an exact correspondence with elements R, T, U in system Y, and for any relation between the elements of system X there is a corresponding relationship between those of system Y. Thus, the relationship of A to B has its exact correspondence in the relationship of R to T, and so on. A map, for example, is an isomorph of certain features of some spherical surface.

When a study of the structure of system X is useful for understanding that of system Y, then X is a model of Y. The isomorphic model is the ideal. Perhaps science progresses at its present rate because isomorphic, mathematical models can be found that correspond to the structure of the physical world.

In a sense, all the explanations dealt with up to now could be expressed in the form of a model. They all presuppose (as indeed does all inference) some representation of relationships between elements in a system; some set of interdependent or interacting parts whose structural principles determine the nature or mutual responsiveness among the parts. The current vogue is to define a model so widely as to embrace any physical or abstract representation of a problem. On this basis, all problem-solving presupposes an implicit or explicit model and any expressed relationships become elements of a model. Even a classification system can be regarded as a model.

It is seldom possible to develop isomorphic models in the world of business; those that are developed are usually oversimplifications. This may be a serious weakness if an understanding of the real world is sacrificed for rigour. On the other hand, a simple model may be sufficient for the purpose; there is always the problem of finding how good a model must be for it to be operationally satisfactory.

There is also the problem of whether to start with a simple model and allow gradually for more realistic assumptions, or to start with the complex and then simplify until the model is manageable. There seems to be no general answer; both approaches have their strengths and weaknesses.

Every manager has models, in the sense that he carries in his head some sort of symbolic representation of how things work. He is apt to classify these models under the heading of experience. He fits day-to-day events into a model and interprets their significance on the basis of this model.

A sales manager may decide after a certain time that a product cannot be successful; how does he know when his efforts to market the product should cease? He has a model (which may not be explicit) which suggests that a potentially successful product should have reached a specific level of sales within a particular time period, given a certain level of promotion. The problem about all such models is that, though the manager has 'guessed' them, he interprets them as an isomorph of the actual situation whereas they merely correspond to a set of hypotheses. Models must preferably be explicit, as they may be a premature organisation of experience. Those that are premature can nevertheless become a framework for thought and exclude other possible models. Northrop has emphasized the importance of the 'natural history stage of inquiry'—the descriptive stage of inquiry to show the diversity and complexity of the occurrences for which any model or theory must account if it is to be adequate. If this stage is ignored the result may be inadequate models that contain more rigour than understanding of the phenomena in question. It is sometimes argued that the pricing models of economists have tended to restrict new approaches. It has also been pointed out that current conceptual models of society, while directing attention to problems of equilibrium, interdependencies and social deviants, neglect the question of sequences.

The aim of management science is to develop better and more explicit models for the manager. However, even where a model is explicit there is a danger that its premises will be ignored and the model confused with reality. Models then become academic toys whose manipulation provides intellectual stimulation but little else. A model does not mirror reality any more than a musical score mirrors the tune. Thus Marshall Walker, a physicist, comments:

'Scientists now find it helpful to use the word model for theories developed long before Bohr emphasized the necessity for this term. To return to our analogy, a scientist no longer feels that he is describing the battle as an eye-witness. The information about the battle comes to him "by telegraph". From this fragmentary information he attempts to construct a map of the battlefield, and on it to move blocks of wood that represent men, companies, and armies. This map and its blocks of wood constitute a material realization of his conceptual model of the battle. The model changes as new information arrives. The scientist observes the changing model, and tries to work out regularities and make predictions. When the model makes many successful predictions, one intuitively expects considerable correspondence between the model and the "thing-out-there", but direct verification is impossible. Except for these correspondences the model need not look at all like the battle.'[1]

There is a danger in wanting, for the purpose of exposition, to give 'flesh and bones' to a model rather than concentrating on structural resemblances. This can be misleading, as Susan Stebbing showed in her criticism of physicists such as Eddington who sought to popularize physics.[2] If a mathematical model accurately predicts, there is no need for any form of visualization.

There is also a danger of management scientists selecting problems, not on the ground of their being pressing to the manager, but because they are potentially researchable in terms of existing models. There is a search here for applications of established models rather than for relevant problems for which theory may have to be developed.

All models need to be tested for internal consistency, over-simplification and over-elaboration (since they cannot be comprehended), and ability to explain and predict. A danger of all models is false analogy. For example, there is always the danger of anthropomorphism in using animals as models for human beings. Frequently the animal model is accepted without indication of the need for evidence drawn from human behaviour. For example, Argyle writes:

[1] Marshall Walker, *The Nature of Scientific Thought*, A Spectrum Book, Prentice-Hall Inc., Englewood Cliffs, N.J., 1963, p. 3.
[2] L. Susan Stebbing, *Philosophy and the Physicists*, Pelican Books, Harmondsworth, 1944.

131

'As with affiliation, sexual motivation is affected by childhood experiences. Harlow found that monkeys reared without mothers or without other infant monkeys did not engage in sexual behaviour in later life . . .'

and

'[Looking] is also emotionally arousing—it has been found that electrical activity in the brain stem of rhesus monkeys increases when humans Look at them.'[1]

Zajonc even claims that the onus is upon others to disprove the suitability of the animal model:

'On the contrary, while human and animal behaviour cannot always be equated, unless we have good *a priori* reasons to believe otherwise, it is best to act as if a generalization made about behaviour applies universally to all species.'[2]

Even if Zajonc's statement had a statistical basis it would not help much in deciding the suitability of the animal model in the individual case. Other evidence would need to be considered, though such evidence would be rooted in observation rather than *a priori* as recommended by Zajonc. (Why we should only be able to refute a model by drawing on statements established independently of observation is a minor mystery.)

Argument by analogy differs from an inductive generalization in that its conclusion is singular rather than general. It may also be said that argument by analogy never proves anything, but only suggests a tentative conclusion.

Supposing X and Y belong to the same general class, argument by analogy proceeds as follows:

1. System X has properties 1, 2 and 3.
2. System Y also has properties 1, 2 and 3.
3. System X also has property 4.
4. Therefore system Y has property 4.

If the two systems X and Y are people who belong to the same general class (e.g. race, students, trade unionists), then argument by analogy can degenerate into stereotyping. Where a subordinate

---

[1] Michael Argyle, *The Psychology of Interpersonal Behaviour*, Pelican Original, Harmondsworth, 1967, pp. 27 and 110.

[2] Robert B. Zajonc, *Social Psychology: An Experimental Approach*, Wadsworth Publishing Co., Belmont, Calif., 1966, p. 17.

quotes precedent as a basis for justifying either his demands (e.g. for his job to be regraded) or his action (e.g. taking it upon himself to refund a customer), he is arguing by analogy. It has then to be decided whether the situations are truly analogous, given the aims and circumstances surrounding the event.

Some points of agreement between two systems is not necessarily evidence for further agreement. The resemblances may be trivial from the point of view of being evidence for the resemblance inferred. Thus, the ability of the floors in the model of a proposed office block to withstand the weight of stanchions and machines does not prove that the floor of the real one will withstand the corresponding weight of real stanchions and real machines. This is the false analogy that results from scaling or moving from the small scale to the large scale. Similarly it can be misleading, for instance, to regard the nervous system as a general model for communications within a business; the cogency of an analogy, like the suitability of a model, demands that the agreement is relevant and the points of difference are irrelevant to the inferences that are made. Allied to false analogy is the fallacy of composition, which commits the error of assuming that what holds true of each member individually is also true of the group generally. Because each division of a company taken individually has maximized its profit, it does not follow that the company as a whole has done so; where divisions are interdependent, more overall profit may be generated if one of the divisions does not seek to maximize its own profit. Similarly, board members competent individually do not necessarily make up an effective board of directors; and the fact that each member of a selection committee has his own bias does not mean that the committee will make a biased selection. On the other hand, the fallacy of division assumes that what is true for the group is also true for each member. Policies that make the company profitable as a whole may result in a loss of efficiency for the individual division. Similarly, a 10% cut in services in every department does not mean that service is reduced to 90% of its former level in each department; the impact in some departments could be disastrous.

TYPES AND PURPOSES OF MODELS

Models in Management

The term 'model' is used in many different senses and no attempt is made here to make an exhaustive list of meanings. We will simply emphasize that the equations which express the models of the economist are of a very different nature from (say) an atomic model.

Models in management serve a number of purposes:

1. Prediction. Thus a mathematical model, establishing functional relationships between dependent and independent variables, is often predictive.
2. Explanation. Models can be an aid to understanding the system they purport to represent simply by their greater familiarity. They can be used to express the qualitative structure of relationships, recognizing that prediction is limited until specific values can be put on the relationships.
3. Heuristic. Models can be an aid to self-discovery. Thus we may manipulate a model to find out what would happen if such and such a relationship were changed, e.g. different inputs of advertising. This is a 'simulation'. If all alternative inputs and structural relationships are tested, this is regarded as exhaustive testing or enumeration, not as simulation. Where the number of alternatives is large, a rule of thumb is necessary to eliminate some of the alternatives. The testing of such a large number of alternatives, albeit restricted by some rule of thumb, is known as 'heuristic programming'; an example is to test the effect on consumer awareness of different amounts of advertising expenditure; limited by the rule that the amounts must cover additional media until the level of awareness reaches (say) thirty per cent of the target audience.

The development of predictive and explanatory models in management science proceeds somewhat as follows:

1. Summary of observations constituting the phenomena to be explained and a tentative selection of relevant variables.
2. Analysis of the data to establish interconnections between the variables, and rearrangement of the data into various possible models that might explain the changes constituting the problem.
3. Analysis of each model for internal consistency, realism and relationship to existing knowledge.
4. Selection of one of the models and the prediction of consequences that will stem from it.
5. Verification by confirming the predicted consequences.

134

Steps 1 and 2 constitute the major problem. Once we have knowledge of the structural principles of some system and of the nature of the elements within it, deduction will show the effect of the structural principles on the system's elements. In geometry, from knowledge of the structural principles of space we can deduce their effect on such elements of space as triangles, circles, straight lines, etc. However, structural principles are not just given, axiomatic or innate to the manager or social scientist. They are essentially empirical 'laws' (e.g. the relationship between advertising and sales) which have to be discovered. Similarly, the precise nature of the variables in the system needs to be found, as the extent to which they are only partly understood limits prediction on how they will interact given the structural principles. Some management scientists pay too little attention to the importance of experience. They behave as if they believed, like the early rationalists,[1] that pure reason reflecting on the problem but acting in an observation vacuum can be a sufficient basis for the development of true belief.

Ackoff sums up the ways a model may be in error as:

'1. The model may contain variables which are not relevant; that is, have no effect on the outcome. Their inclusion in the model, then, makes the predicted outcome depend on factors on which it has no dependence in reality.'

'2. The model may not include variables which are relevant; that is, ones that do affect the outcome.

'3. The function, f, which relates the controllable and uncontrollable variables to the outcome may be incorrect.'

'4. The numerical values assigned to the variables may be inaccurate.'[2]

Management scientists classify models in many different ways. Thus, models differ on the basis of structure, and distinctions can be made between: symbolic models, where properties are represented by symbols as in the mathematical model; iconic models which are just scaled-down versions of the real thing; and analogue models

[1] It was early recognized that sensibility and reason were the two major faculties by which we acquired knowledge. The problem was to determine the role of each. The rationalists (Descartes, Spinoza, Leibniz), generalizing from mathematics, favoured pure reason working in almost complete independence of the senses. The empiricists (Locke, Berkeley, Hume) argued that true belief must be based on reflection on sense experience and that reason alone was sterile.

[2] Russell L. Ackoff, *Scientific Method*, John Wiley & Sons Inc., New York, 1968, pp. 139–40.

where, say, a liquid is used to represent the flow of money in the economy. Another common distinction is between static and dynamic models. Static models do not consider effects through time. Dynamic models do, as they seek to predict change from changes currently taking place.

Theories in Science

Laws or generalizations relating to some subject matter must be mutually supporting. When a group of laws or hypotheses forms a system to explain a phenomenon, the system is called a *'formal'* theory. Laws must be deducible from the theory, though the deduction may not be direct but require translation of the laws into the vocabulary of the theory.

The term 'model' is often used by many management scientists to embrace the concept of theory, hypothesis and law. However, a distinction can be made between a model and a theory. Models are generally constructed to solve some specific problem, rather than to solve types of problems. When a model is examined its structural properties are emphasized, but in the studying of a formal theory the substantive content of its propositions receives prominence. A theory is much more embracing than any corresponding model. Models would be deducible from their corresponding theories, but would not exhaust the content of the theories.

There may be several models to represent the same basic theory or some basic law. To be adequate a theory must suggest the interrelationships which collectively constitute the model. In fact, difficulty in subsuming hypotheses under some theory often lies not in devising an all-embracing proposition, but in devising a theory to imply a model that interrelates the hypotheses. Thus a theory T that is merely the equivalent of joining together hypotheses $H_1, H_2 \ldots H_n$ is of little practical significance; it must interrelate hypotheses, so that the evidence for the truth of one provides some evidence for the truth of the others, and is likely in consequence to suggest more hypotheses. There can also, of course, be models for theories, in the sense that the model is an heuristic device which can be used to arrive at hypotheses leading to laws and theories.

A theory does not so much mirror reality as show one aspect of it revealed in the concepts, properties and variables which it selects and relates. A theory will contain certain primitive terms; their meaning is taken for granted as they remain undefined, or at least they are given meaning derived syntactically from the postulates of the theory in which they occur. The primitive terms are used to define the 'derived' concepts from which the hypotheses in the theory are constructed. Some of these hypotheses can be regarded as postulates if all other hypotheses in the theory can be inferred from them.

Theories themselves can be checked by confirming deduced consequences. Thus the theorems deduced from the postulates of physics can be confirmed experimentally. However, because of the nature of economic phenomena, many of the postulates of economic science are taken to be axiomatic, and theorems are confirmed simply by showing them to follow from the postulates. Hence Harold Laski's remark that economics consisted merely of exercises in deduction. This is perhaps only partly true of economics today, as much use is made of statistical analysis, though experimentation is not considered practical.

An event is isolated until explained by a law, but a law is isolated until subsumed under some theory. Evidence for the truth of a law that is part of a theory, is composed not only of that collected in confirming the law, but also of evidence supporting other laws in the theory. It is because of this that a finding that seemingly contradicts some established law does not lead to the law being suspected first; the finding is more likely to be examined in the first instance. Similarly, an hypothesis (e.g. the desire for participation) derived as a possible corollary to some theory (e.g. Maslow's theory of needs) will be accepted on less evidence than one isolated from other theoretical knowledge; an hypothesis that fits into an existing theory can be just as acceptable as one that is confirmed by observation.

Ackoff makes a useful distinction between scientific tools, techniques and methods. The word 'tool' he restricts to 'physical or conceptual instruments' such as computers and tables of logarithms. 'Techniques' he regards as ways of using the scientific tools, while he reserves the term 'method' for the procedures used to select the technique. A problem that can be completely solved by applying some technique can be regarded as routine and the decision as a programmed one. Techniques can establish relationships but the explanatory nature and value of those relationships are established by laws and theories. Relationships that cannot be explained do not inspire confidence in their use.

137

Theories in Social Science

The word 'theory' is often used more loosely than as defined above. It is commonly employed to denote a set of hypotheses and may not be distinguished from the term 'model'. In this sense we all have informal theories, in the same way that we have informal models. These may determine what we observe, the manner in which we analyse data collected, and the explanations we accept or offer for the problems that arise from day to day. Such informal theories and models help to systematize and explain observations and events, and represent the organization of past experience. But there is always the danger that such organization is premature.

Many social scientists believe that much research consists merely of demonstrating statistical relationships rather than establishing explanations. Alternatively, a problem is tackled that is merely a special case of some wider problem. Why not research the wider problem from the start? The answer that the wider problem would outstrip resources and take too long invites the suggestion that the individual research should contribute towards testing the wider theory.

The term 'theory' is being used in social science to indicate propositions developed to suggest hypotheses, rather than to synthesize and systematize existing corroborated hypotheses. Such 'over-arching' theories do not have so much evidence that they can be accepted as dogma. They result more from systematic reflection than from any attempt to interrelate established regularities. The reason for their emergence is to give some direction to research from the start of inquiry. Thus we have several such theories to account for attitude change, though all stress the acquisition of attitudes by experience.

In the perceptual approach (e.g. that of Asch) an attitude is altered by changing the subject's perception of the event, object or situation; the object referent remains the same, but its connotative meaning changes. The learning theory approach (e.g. that of Hovland) stresses the effect of some variable on attitude through learning. Here an attitude change occurs because new information leads the subject to change his opinion about the event, object or situation. The emphasis is on the response to the stimulus, not on the perception of it. The approach of the various consistency theories (e.g. that of Festinger) stresses that attitudes are changed in order to achieve consistency between the beliefs themselves and overt behaviour. Finally, in the functional theory the emphasis is on changing the perceived instrumentality of the object to the subject's needs.

These theories are difficult to confirm in their entirety, yet they serve a useful purpose. Social science has a wealth of empirical findings, but seldom any framework in which to put the various findings together. Since facts uninterpreted by theory often beg as many questions as they explain, it appears to some social scientists that the broad theory must be developed first so as to suggest hypotheses which may lead to a modified and truer theory.

NORMATIVE THEORY

The term 'normative theory' is used to specify some ideal, e.g. that of democratic government. Northrop points out that normative theory does not claim to have an exact counterpart in reality, and should not be validated as if it did.

'One does not take it as argument against the Christian ideal for life that there are no perfect Christians. Yet, if normative social theories were handled by the same methods as those used for factual social theories, this is precisely what we should conclude when we find our normative social theories to be out of accord with specific facts in any actual society.'[1]

Northrop argues that, if a normative theory were to be verified by the methods of natural science, it would have to be in complete accord with some actual state of affairs. He asserts that normative theory should be confirmed by checking whether its postulates and primitive ideas are in accord with those of verified natural science.

Several questions can be raised here. What are these verified, irrefutable, unambiguous findings of science to which we should all adhere? Many of us who feel that a belief in birth control is consistent with the postulates of science, do not find this a convincing argument when used against those whose faith teaches them otherwise. Even if we were to accept Northrop's method, how many normative theories could be checked this way? It is also difficult to see why it is untenable to speculate about the consequences of having achieved

[1] F. S. C. Northrop, *The Logic of the Sciences and the Humanities*, Meridian Books, The World Publishing Co., New York, 1959, p. 21

the normative objective, and to argue that this would be disastrous for other values held. Values are goals in terms of human need, and as such are both multiple and conflicting. Some values that are meant to be instrumental in achieving higher values may become ends in themselves. Hence values need to be examined. They can often be given some objective base by seeking out the higher value premises that lie behind particular judgments and determining as a whole the consequences of maintaining such values. In other words, values often need to be justified in terms of likely consequences, either for the person himself or as seen for the population at large. Rapoport argues that there are four invariant needs of man: the need for survival, the need to belong, the need for order, and the need for security. He argues that there is no point in seeking to justify values if they directly pursue these needs.

> 'It is sensible to ask, "Is the pursuit of power good?" or "Is the pursuit of knowledge good?" if these questions lead to an investigation of how the pursuit of knowledge or of power is related to the invariant needs, such as those of survival or security. But it makes no sense to ask, "Is the pursuit of security good?" if it is found that the pursuit of security in one form or another is universal.
>
> 'In short, it is sensible to evaluate the ethical implications of the means used in the pursuit of the goals but not of the goals themselves.'[1]

Coductionism

The question may arise as to the status of these various types of explanation: are some more fundamental than others? Kurtz regards these different explanations as if they were merely different facets of a problem. He argues for what he terms 'coductionism', in which each type of explanation makes its contribution to understanding at different levels of interpretation. Thus, in explaining conflict in an organization, we might use several methods:

1. State who caused what, in the sense of attributing blame for the resulting state of affairs, or demonstrate what is actionable to remedy the situation; whether treating 'who is responsible' as

[1] Anatol Rapoport, *Operational Philosophy*, John Wiley & Sons Inc., New York, 1953, p. 97.

a cause confuses the search for cause with the problem of ethics is a matter of dispute.

2. Explain by means of a model or theory built around such propositions as 'when competition is unregulated by rules, it degenerates into conflict'.
3. Showing the divergent goals and motives of each of the participants in the conflict.
4. Showing the role that conflict plays in bringing about change.
5. Trace the history of the conflict at some point in time to show how the various actions taken by the participants led up to the present position.

Coductionism is the viewpoint that seems most useful for current decision-making, though there are others. The reductionist aims at reducing each macro-science to some micro-science. This is something more than subsuming one theory into a wider theory, as would occur if current leadership theory were explained in terms of current interpersonal influence theory. The aim would be to reduce biology and psychology to physics or, as in methodological individualism, to reduce all the social sciences to biology and psychology. Another view is that each science develops to cope with different levels of phenomena, and has theories formulated at different levels of abstraction. Thus Morris argues that psychology (dealing with personality), sociology (dealing with social phenomena), and anthropology (dealing with culture) are 'irreducible sub-systems of human action'.[1] Reductionism may be ignoring the fact that the macro-system is not simply the sum of its micro-elements, and that new laws may need to be developed for the macro-level.

While some argue for different levels of explanation, others argue for particular forms of explanation. Currently there are those who, in the words of Kaplan, find 'the mathematical model the respository of all wisdom'.

[1] Charles Morris, *Signification and Significance*, M.I.T. Press, Cambridge, Mass., 1964.

141

Chapter 9

PREDICTIVE DECISION

EXPLANATION AND PREDICTION

Prediction refers to future events, as opposed to explanation which argues about the nature of current or past events. More specifically, prediction focuses on the effects of a set of events, while explanation seeks the conditions that are functionally related to the events.

In general, the better we are able to explain what has happened within some system, the better we can predict what will happen. This has led some writers to regard explanation and prediction as logically isomorphic, so that 'to be able to explain is to be able to predict correctly'. Perhaps much depends on how broadly we are expected to predict. Evolutionary theory constitutes an explanation which may predict consequences in terms of future archaeological findings, but it does not claim to accurately predict the future evolutionary pattern of man. Scheffler points out that prediction does not necessitate explanation, though he believes explanation does contain some prediction:

> 'The point then is that, in the usual sense of "prediction", not every restatement of a prediction after the event is explanatory, even though every statement of an explanation prior to the event is predictive . . .
>
> 'Explanations are true, predictions need not be; making predictions is part of one way of confirming the existence of explanations; predictions may be made with or without rational grounds, and some rational grounds adequate for prediction fail to explain the predicted occurrences.'[1]

Explanation does not always allow accurate prediction, it does not necessarily incorporate all the necessary and sufficient conditions for a prediction to be made. On the other hand, the grounds on

[1] Israel Scheffler 'Explanation, Prediction and Abstraction' in *Philosophy of Science*, ed. Arthur Danto and Sidney Morgenbesser, Meridian Books, The World Publishing Co., New York, 1966, pp. 277 and 280.

142

which some occurrence is predicted do not necessarily provide an explanation of it.

Prediction argues from evidence, as opposed to prophecy which has a mystic basis. Prediction without explanation is tested for the degree to which the process used to predict has been valid in the past. This process is mainly statistical and can be tested only by its past performance. Prediction without an explanatory base may be perfectly adequate for many purposes, particularly if it is intended to adapt to the predicted future rather than attempt to change it. A prediction with an explanation is based on some model of reality, and this implies an understanding of the basic underlying system. It also suggests the possibility of control rather than acceptance of the predicted future as unchangeable. The explanatory model is tested by examining the assumptions on which it is based and the values placed on the interrelationships among the variables forming its structure; it is also tested for its past performance, and is the more basic predictive tool.

A prediction in itself can influence events. Giving publicity to a prediction may in itself bring about the prediction, in that without such publicity it would not come true. Thus the prediction by top management that a certain employee is likely to rise to the top may be a 'self-fulfilling prophecy' if they are in a position to bring it about. Also, as our background of experience helps to frame our expectations, our perceptions become selective so that we see what we want. In a way this resembles the self-fulfilling prophecy. The interviewer after reading a candidate's job application may have certain expectations that tend to be realized through selective perception. Similarly, publicity may vitiate some prediction, as publishing the prediction may change the set of conditions that gave rise to it. For example, the announcement by management of very profitable years ahead may be 'suicidal', by leading to increased wage demands and soaring share prices.

There can be no certainty in prediction. Even where laws can be used as bases for prediction they do not necessarily ensure accuracy, since all the necessary conditions for the law to apply may not be present in the future. However, we will not deal with prediction as an exercise in mathematical logic—that is, where the prediction is simply implied by some law or theory. But what of predictions other than the implications of laws? We must choose between the following alternatives.

1. Any form of prediction is ruled out.
2. Prediction can only be made from some general principle that is taken as being certain. This is not really tenable since, however carefully some rule is applied, the results are never the same on all occasions; some error is left to be explained.
3. Generalizations from experience can give predictions with some degree of probability but are by no means certain.

How do we justify inductive prediction? There is no way of guaranteeing that a prediction will be true, because we cannot ensure that the assumptions supporting prediction will hold true in the future. However, it is possible to lend support to inductive predictions on the basis of probability. A short discussion on calculating probabilities is first required.

Joint Probability

When the probability of one event is $P(A)$ and that of another event is $P(B)$, then the probability of both events occurring if they are unrelated is $P(A) \times P(B)$. Thus the probability of getting a tail in tossing an unbiased coin is $\frac{1}{2}$ and the chance of getting a 2 in tossing a die is $\frac{1}{6}$. Therefore the probability of getting a tail and a 2 if both coin and die were tossed is

$$P(AB) = P(A) \times P(B) = \tfrac{1}{2} \times \tfrac{1}{6} = \tfrac{1}{12}$$

But events are sometimes connected. Suppose a bag contains 5 red and 3 black balls. Then the probability of drawing one red ball is $\frac{5}{8}$, but the probability of drawing two red balls is

$$\frac{5}{8} \times \frac{4}{7} = \frac{20}{56} = 0.36,$$

since after the first red ball is drawn only 7 balls remain of which 4 are red. Symbolically, the joint probability for events that are statistically dependent (such as the probability of getting two red balls) is

$$P(AB) = P(A) \times P(B|A)$$

Conditional Probability

In the example above, the probability of drawing a red ball after one red was already drawn was $P(B|A) = \frac{4}{7}$. The probability of picking a second red ball is dependent on what happens at the first drawing, and is known as the 'conditional probability' of drawing a second red after one red has been drawn.

Since $P(AB) = P(A) \times P(B|A)$, then the conditional probability is

$$P(B|A) = \frac{P(AB)}{P(A)}$$

In the example above, $P(B|A) = \frac{4}{9}$.

Alternative Probability

The probability that one of several possible, mutually exclusive ways will happen is the sum of the probabilities of the separate events:

$$P(A \text{ or } B) = P(A) + P(B)$$

Thus the probability of drawing either an ace, a ten of diamonds or a two of spades is

$$\frac{4}{52} + \frac{1}{52} + \frac{1}{52} = \frac{6}{52}$$

In certain instances events may not be mutually exclusive, that is, both may occur. In this case the probability that either one will occur or both is

$$P(A \text{ or } B) = P(A) + P(B) - P(AB)$$

If the probability of getting rain tomorrow is 0·4, and that of getting sunshine is 0·8 and the probability of both rain and sunshine is 0·4, then the probability of getting either rain or sunshine is

$$P(A \text{ or } B) = 0·4 + 0·8 - 0·4 = 0·8$$

The various probability formulas so far discussed are shown in Table 4.

BAYESIAN INFERENCE

A prediction results from some hypothesis, and the validity of that prediction is related to the probability with which the hypothesis is true. New information can revise probabilities by the use of Bayes's theorem, which is simply conditional probability and extensions of that concept.

Essential to an understanding of Bayes's theorem in its broader aspects is the idea of total probability. Suppose we have two

K

mutually exclusive and exhaustive events, A and not-A ($\bar{A}$). For example, $P(A)$ could be the probability of a machine being loaded properly, while $P(\bar{A})$ could be the probability of its not being loaded properly. Since the events are exhaustive and mutually exclusive,

$$P(A) + P(\bar{A}) = 1$$

If $P(B)$ represents the probability of getting a good product from the machine, then $P(B|A)$ is the probability of getting a good product given that the machine is properly loaded, and $P(B|\bar{A})$ is the probability of getting a good product given that the machine is not properly loaded.

Table 4

Type of Probability	Symbol	Formula	
		Statistical independence	Statistical dependence
Joint	$P(AB)$	$P(A) \times P(B)$	$P(B) \times P(A/B)$ or $P(A) \times P(B/A)$
Conditional	$P(B|A)$	$P(B)$	$P(AB)/P(A)$
		Mutually exclusive	Not mutually exclusive
Alternative	$P(A$ or $B)$	$P(A) + P(B)$	$P(A) + P(B) - P(AB)$

Let us assume the following values:

$$P(A) = 0.7, \qquad P(B|A) = 0.9,$$
$$P(\bar{A}) = 0.3, \qquad P(B|\bar{A}) = 0.1.$$

Then the joint probability of both getting a good product and loading the machine properly is

$$P(A) \times P(B|A) = 0.7 \times 0.9 = 0.63,$$

and the joint probability of both getting a good product and not loading the machine properly is

$$P(\bar{A}) \times P(B|\bar{A}) = 0.3 \times 0.1 = 0.03.$$

The total probability of getting a good product, by the rule for alternative probability (mutually exclusive events), is

$$P(A) \times P(B|A) + P(\bar{A}) \times P(B|\bar{A}) = 0.63 + 0.03$$
$$= 0.66.$$

If we now receive information that the machine has produced a good product, we can revise the probability of the machine being properly loaded.

$P(A|B)$ is the probability of the machine being properly loaded given the new information that it has produced a good product.

The conditional probability formula states that

$$P(A|B) = \frac{P(AB)}{P(B)}.$$

But

$$P(AB) = P(B) \times P(A|B) = P(A) \times P(B|A)$$

and

$$P(B) = \text{Total probability of getting a good product}$$
$$= P(A) \times P(B|A) + P(\bar{A}) \times P(B|\bar{A}),$$

so that

$$P(A|B) = \frac{P(AB)}{P(B)} = \frac{P(A) \times P(B|A)}{P(B)} =$$
$$\frac{P(A) \times P(B|A)}{P(A) \times P(B|A) + P(\bar{A}) \times P(B|\bar{A})} = \frac{0.63}{0.66} = 0.95.$$

The revised probability 0.95 now replaces 0.7, which was the initial probability for the machine being loaded properly.

We can use the same procedure to reconsider our choice of some hypothesis in the light of new information. Suppose we have four mutually exclusive and exhaustive hypotheses, A, B, C, D, and that hypothesis A has been the one favoured to date. In fact, probabilities are as follows:

$$P(A) = 0.4,$$
$$P(B) = 0.3,$$
$$P(C) = 0.2,$$
$$P(D) = 0.1.$$

In the light of the new data, Z, the conditional probabilities of Z relative to each of the hypotheses are:

$$P(Z|A) = 0.1,$$
$$P(Z|B) = 0.5,$$

147

$$P(Z|C) = 0\cdot2,$$
$$P(Z|D) = 0\cdot2.$$

The following would be the four revised probabilities:

1. The revised probability of hypothesis A given the new information Z is

$$P(A|Z) = \frac{(0\cdot4)\,(0\cdot1)}{(0\cdot4)\,(0\cdot1)+(0\cdot5)\,(0\cdot3)+(0\cdot2)\,(0\cdot2)+(0\cdot1)\,(0\cdot2)}$$

$$= \frac{0\cdot04}{0\cdot25} = 0\cdot16.$$

2. The revised probability of hypothesis B given the new information Z is

$$P(B|Z) = \frac{(0\cdot5)\,(0\cdot3)}{0\cdot25} = \frac{0\cdot15}{0\cdot25} = 0\cdot6.$$

3. The revised probability of hypothesis C given the new information Z is

$$P(C|Z) = \frac{(0\cdot2)\,(0\cdot2)}{0\cdot25} = \frac{0\cdot04}{0\cdot25} = 0\cdot16.$$

4. The revised probability of hypothesis D given the new information Z is

$$P(D|Z) = \frac{(0\cdot1)\,(0\cdot2)}{0\cdot25} = \frac{0\cdot02}{0\cdot25} = 0\cdot08.$$

Although hypothesis A was the one initially selected as being the most probable, B would now be selected.

The above process is known as Bayesian inference. The probabilities with which we start are progressively revised as we receive new information.

A problem lies in determining the basic given probabilities. Essentially these are estimates based on experience or derived through some form of analogy with similar hypotheses and types of outcomes. Such 'guess-estimating' may be difficult to accept, but the initial probabilities matter less as new evidence emerges to revise them.

Any prediction is composed of three sets of components and is developed from assumptions about them.

1. In the first set there is an assumption that certain elements will not change except between statistical chance limits within the time period covered by the prediction. These 'background constants' will persist because their inherent characteristics dictate this conclusion with a high degree of confidence. Thus, in making predictions for the next six months, it may be confidently assumed that income distribution, religious beliefs and so on will not alter for the nation as a whole.

2. The second set of components relate to statistical trends. Trends can be identified from time series and projected into the future. Such trend projections are not just 'a projection of ignorance' if reasons for them can be identified. Of course, the greater the projection, the greater the uncertainty about the likelihood of a turning-point, but, as the success of insurance companies testifies, past trends can be expected to continue within acceptable limits of error.

3. The final set of components refers to those elements that show sudden and abrupt change. Even components that were thought to represent 'background constants' or whose trend could be predicted, may fall into this category. The attitudes of the inhabitants of a country can change almost overnight towards a country with which they find themselves suddenly at war. Similarly, birth rate trends may suddenly change during a depression, and so on. Even here however, there may be prediction. Sudden change may simply represent the termination of some process, or may simply be the result of man-made plans which can be discovered in advance. Thus the film industry could have anticipated a reduction in audiences with the proposed introduction of television, and businesses could predict that government spending on armaments would decrease with the end of a war or a lessening of world tension.

TECHNOLOGICAL FORECASTING

Prediction in practice is a mixture of trend extrapolation and prediction from some explanatory base. This can be illustrated by technological forecasting which, as the name implies, is concerned with predicting likely advances in technology and science and acting as a basis for giving direction to research and development, etc.

A chart of the main techniques is shown in Fig. 16. The first

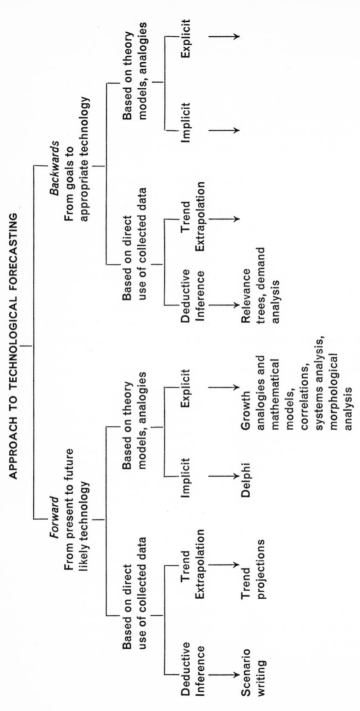

APPROACH TO TECHNOLOGICAL FORECASTING

Forward
From present to future likely technology

Based on direct use of collected data

Deductive Inference → Scenario writing

Trend Extrapolation → Trend projections

Based on theory models, analogies

Implicit → Delphi

Explicit → Growth analogies and mathematical models, correlations, systems analysis, morphological analysis

Backwards
From goals to appropriate technology

Based on direct use of collected data

Deductive Inference → Relevance trees, demand analysis

Trend Extrapolation →

Based on theory models, analogies

Implicit →

Explicit →

Figure 16

basis of division is the direction of forecasting. The forecaster can start from the existing state of technology, or begin with the establishment of a goal and try to predict how the goal will be achieved.

Whether forecasting is forwards or backwards from goals, it can again be subclassified depending on whether it is based on empirical data or purely on theory. If the forecasting is based on empirical data it can be developed either by deductive inference or by trend extrapolation. If it is based on a theory or model, the theory can be either implicit or explicit.

Scenario Writing Technique

This approach has been used by Herman Kahn and his associates at the Hudson Institute, New York. Starting from some described state of technology, the approach deduces step by step the logical evolution. What paths and terminal points are possible and likely? How could some hypothetical situation come about? The forecaster seeks not so much to predict but to explore the alternative directions possible and the problems likely to arise.

Trend Projections

This treats progress as a function of time and assumes that the same forces operating in the past will continue along the same pattern in the future.

Delphi Technique

This approach was developed by Olaf Helmer at the Rand Corporation. It can be viewed as a way of tapping the opinions of groups of experts while avoiding the possibility of bias that might arise through bringing them together to interact. The procedure is as follows:

1. The experts are asked to list what developments are likely in their field during the next, say, twenty years or to name inventions or other breakthroughs urgently needed and feasible.
2. In the next round, the experts are asked for probable dates of events predicted.
3. In the third round, the data is fed back to the experts. They note where a consensus has been reached, and dissidents are asked to give their reasons. This gives all an opportunity to reconsider their opinions, and the forecaster a chance to re-phrase ambiguities in his questions.

4. In round four, the experts are again given the consensus and minority opinions, and are asked to record again their estimates of when the events are likely and very likely.

The method by which the experts arrive at their forecasts is left to them, though being 'experts' one would expect them to base their forecasts on something more than mere trend extrapolation.

Growth Analogies

For example, a substitution growth curve suggests that substitution of one technology for another follows the S-shaped fashion curve—slow at first, faster as acceptance grows, then tapering off as saturation is approached. There must be evidence that the curve is appropriate before it is used in market forecasting. Thus past history must show that the curve is evolving and that further substitution appears to be feasible.

Correlated Events

There may be a correlation between one predictable event and the event to be predicted, e.g. military aircraft speeds may be a guide to future airliner speeds.

Systems Analysis

A study of man-machine systems may show weaknesses, and a study of the appropriate technology may suggest paths by which the weaknesses can be overcome. Systems analysts may also define future problems and the characteristics of the technology needed to solve them.

Morphological Analysis

Here it is hoped to produce insight by reflection on form and structure. The problem is first broadly defined and then the independent variables of the desired system are listed. For example, two such variables for a television would be colour and shape of picture. The different values these variables could assume are then noted. For a television there could be 3 colours of picture: black and white, single colour and full colour, and 3 shapes of picture: round, oval, and rectangular. The number of possible combinations —each forming a possible solution—is given by multiplying the values together. Thus, if there were just the two independent variables of colour and shape, there would be $3 \times 3 = 9$ different possible combinations or possible systems which could be explored for technological possibilities. This technique was developed by a Swiss astronomer Fritz Zwicky for systematically exploring all technological opportunities.

Relevance Trees

This technique starts with the establishment of goals and opportunities. The technological alternatives are then traced to a number of steps which represent deficiencies in the existing state of technology, Methods have been developed for assigning priorities to research. An example of this technique is Honeywell's 'pattern' (Planning, Assistance Through Technical Evaluation of Relevance Numbers).

Demand Assessments

It is argued that need is the basic spur to technological developments. Hence the basic problem is to identify urgent future needs through (say) demographic and sociological analysis, e.g. pollution.

Governments were the first to adopt technological forecasting, but it has spread rapidly among larger companies who usually supplement their forecasting staffs by outside consultants or research institutions. The techniques have had notable success in spite of the fact that the inference process of the various techniques is inadequately documented.

Chapter 10

EVALUATIVE DECISION

All decision involves some evaluation, as decision involves selection and with selection there is always evaluation. In an evaluative decision, the decision-maker is concerned with the decision whose immediate goal is to rank the value of a set of items according to some criterion. His aim is to determine their relative worth or contribution to objectives.

A decision-maker may evaluate past performance or future potential. The latter alternative involves prediction of consequences, that rankings on the criteria will correlate highly with future performance in promoting goals. On the other hand, evaluation of past performance involves comparison of actual performance against criteria to determine the degree of attainment. In either case, a criteria may allow division into categories, one of which may be labelled 'standard' to represent satisfactory performance. This may consitute the basis for some system of control. In the absence of a predetermined standard, whether a particular score on some criterion represents a good or poor performance may be a matter of opinion. In interpreting figures, there is a need for standards to act as controls. It is difficult to know how to interpret many figures in market research (e.g. 'the mean age of buyers is thirty' or 'twenty per cent do not repeat buy') unless there is some norm against which a comparison can be made. Often 'norms' are too subjective, being based on analogous but perhaps misleading experience. There is evidence that in judging others we use ourselves as the norm so that, for example, secure people are more likely to see others as 'warm' than as 'cold' personalities and so on.

Every evaluation is in terms of some set of values or objectives which form a criterion against which evaluation can be made. If we accept, for the purpose of argument, that profit maximization is the ultimate aim of a business, then all activities in a business should be evaluated on the basis of their contribution to profit. The ideal

154

result of evaluating a set of items would be to rank them in order of their profit contribution. In the case of evaluating courses of action, this procedure requires that the consequences of each alternative can be predicted and measured in terms of likely profit contribution, as illustrated by the payoff matrix concept to be discussed in the next chapter. But the problems of evaluation are usually not so simple.

MEASUREMENT OF OBJECTIVES

Profit is seldom put forward without constraints as the sole goal, and there is the problem of measuring attainment in objectives when attainment is not a matter of all or nothing.

1. Values can act as constraints on the profit motive, as when a company sacrifices growth and profit to retain family ownership or, for instance, as the British building firm Wates refuses to extend operations to South Africa because of apartheid. The role of values as a determinant of top policy is often obscured by wording that suggests the problem of selecting objectives is merely technical. For example, 'Which set of objectives and policies will make the company the most profitable?' suggests that the problem is one of searching for the alternative that most promotes profit, whereas a solution on this criterion alone might suggest goals that are rejected on grounds emanating from unstated value premises.

2. There is difficulty in making the concept of profit operational. Profit interpretation as a rate of return for capital employed is particularly misleading, as it ignores the scale of operations. For example, a divisional manager with some freedom to determine investment could maximize rate of return by actually restricting divisional growth and reducing overall corporate profit. Further problems are those of trade-off between profit and risk and of determining the period over which profit is to be calculated. For example, the full consequences of the decisions and actions by divisional management are not immediately reflected in divisional profits. That item on the liabilities side of a balance sheet entitled 'net profit' can be a poor guide to yearly performance. A divisional general manager may inflate profits for several years by practices that might be detrimental to the company in the long term; an obvious example is to cut out expenditure that will not immediately affect profits (e.g. expenditure on maintenance, research and

development, and advertising), though a long-term view might show such expenditure to be justified. The selling of building and other assets that have appreciated well beyond their book value is another means of artificially keeping profits high in the short run. On the other hand, the man who incurs expenditure from which the benefits will only accrue in the future may have a low performance, if the criterion is based simply on the level of annual profits.

Even where rate of return is not used and the more sophisticated concept of residual net income (net earnings less cost of capital) is adopted, the question arises of determining what is to be included or excluded from net earnings. A division can be shown during any financial year to have made a whole range of possible earnings, depending on the system used to measure them: the recorded earnings of a division can be inflated or depressed by the use of different accounting procedures, company policies and divisional practices.[1]

Our objectives are usually multiple and conflicting, and there is real difficulty in making them operational. We may argue that 'success on the job' is the objective in selecting job applicants. Finding a measure of success is particularly complex, especially when the abilities required for the immediate job are negatively related to those for the job one level higher.

Sometimes, to make objectives operational, only the part that is easy to measure (e.g. cost reduction) is put forward to assess achievement on the total set of objectives. For example, market share might be used erroneously as a surrogate indicator of profitability, or the standard of living as a measure of the quality of life generally. In fact, the belief that measurable objectives reflect all objectives may lead to the efficient solution of the wrong problem.

NEED FOR INTERMEDIATE GOALS

Even if profit were an adequate objective and could be made operational, it would not be always possible to estimate the contribution of every activity to profit; the contribution of advertising, for example, is difficult to assess, because its effects cannot usually be distinguished from those of other elements in the marketing mix. In any case, ultimate objectives may only be attainable in the long run, as, for example, in the case of research and development.

[1] See David Solomons, *Divisional Performance: Measurement and Control*, Financial Executives Research Foundation, New York, 1965.

156

All this means that objectives other than ultimate ones must usually form a criterion for evaluation. These can be called intermediate objectives or criteria. The intermediate objectives for evaluating some advertising campaign can be formulated in terms of creating awareness and forming a favourable attitude.

The need for intermediate objectives (or criteria) raises an evaluation problem of its own, associated with establishing the relevance of intermediate to ultimate objectives. Does a high contribution to intermediate objectives lead to a high performance on ultimate objectives? We cannot always demonstrate a high positive relationship between intermediate and ultimate objectives, e.g. between relative attitudes to brands and related purchases. Thus, intermediate goals may not further ultimate objectives, with the danger that instrumental means become ends in themselves.

The extent to which intermediate objectives are *deficient* as goals is the extent to which they fail to fully capture ultimate objectives. The extent to which they are *relevant* is the extent to which they overlap ultimate objectives. Finally, the extent to which intermediate objectives are *contaminated* is the extent to which intermediate objectives are unrelated to ultimate objectives.

We should not conclude from what has been said that ultimate objectives, where it is possible to use them, should always be used exclusively. Additional intermediate objectives may be used to remind subordinates how best to achieve ultimate ones. Thus, emphasis might be placed on how a salesman carries out merchandizing, even though he can be assessed accurately on the final objective of profit contribution. In this way attention is focused on factors that determine the final result. Also, the measurement of attainment on such intermediary goals can facilitate an analysis of reasons for any departure from standard.

Ultimate objectives are usually made up of a number of independent factors. For example, the object of efficiency is composed, not only of output and quality factors, but also of factors such as accident rates, absenteeism and employee motivation. As each factor is assessed independently they may be brought together, through weighting, into an overall index. Weighting should be on the basis of contribution to ultimate objectives. But precise measurement is seldom possible so reliance is placed on judgment or, through trial and error, trying to get out weights that give the best fit to some measure of achievement on ultimate objectives. However,

157

such a weighting system can be arbitrary and illegitimate and can fail to take into account that weights should change as trade-offs change with degrees of attainment.

DETERMINING THE RELEVANT ATTRIBUTES TO BE EVALUATED

The attributes of items are evaluated, and those selected will depend on the objectives to be achieved. Thus in personnel selection the attributes evaluated are those which are considered relevant to job success. A job analysis is the basis for a job description. In turn, a job description forms the basis for a job specification that lists the traits needed, viz:

(a) morphological traits, e.g. height and weight
(b) physiological traits, e.g. blood pressure
(c) aptitudes, e.g. scholastic aptitude
(d) achievement
(e) disposition ⎤
(f) drives   ⎮
(g) interests   ⎬ personality traits
(h) values   ⎮
(i) attitudes   ⎦

DETERMINING OPERATIONAL DEFINITIONS OF ATTRIBUTES

As another illustration we might take the evaluation of a supervisor. We may argue that the following attributes are relevant to his success:

(a) considerate
(b) firm leadership
(c) supportive of the company and his subordinates
(d) administrative ability.

All these constructs which may be relevant to success as a supervisor need to be spelled out and defined operationally. An interviewer asked to choose the applicant with the most 'drive' will have his own interpretation of this word in the absence of an operational definition. In the case of scientific constructs, operational definitions will stem from the theory of which the construct is part.

There is often a problem in justifying the selection of particular characteristics as being most relevant to the attributes or constructs of interest. Inferences from traits to behaviour may be made on any of three bases.

1. *Theory or model.* Different theories or models will involve different operational definitions. Construct validity really depends on accepting the theory, as the meaning of the constructs are embodied in its postulates. As Cronbach and Meehl point out, if to one investigator aggressiveness means overt assault on others, and if another uses the same term to include repressed hostile reactions, the two will not agree on what tests measure aggressiveness.[1]

2. *Judgment.* Judgment may be the sole basis for a claim that a certain type of behaviour indicates a certain trait. For instance, referees attribute personality traits to people purely on the basis of their own judgment.

3. *Factor analysis.* As this approach determines which set of behaviours co-vary, it is argued that only those sub-sets of behaviour responses that always go together are descriptive of the trait. Of course, the name given to the sub-set depends on deciding what each member of the sub-set has in common.

DETERMINING OPERATIONAL MEASURES OF RELEVANT ATTRIBUTES

We may need not only an operational definition, but also an operational measure of the relevant attribute. Thus a superior, asked to rank his subordinates on the basis of productivity, may have to rely on his impressions, if measures of output are not available. In fact, operational measures are taken as essential for most assessment purposes. For example, we do not simply list the responses made by an interviewee to an attitude questionnaire; we try to scale or measure these responses.

In Likert's summated rating scale, the respondent is asked to indicate degree of agreement or disagreement with some statement reflecting the attitude in question:

(a) agree very strongly   (7)

[1] L. J. Cronbach and P. E. Meehl, 'Construct Validity in Psychological Tests', *Psychological Bulletin*, July 1955.

(b) agree strongly   (6)
(c) agree   (5)
(d) disagree   (3)
(e) disagree strongly   (2)
(f) disagree very strongly   (1)
(Note: 'no response' is given a score of 4).

The score in parentheses are used to reflect intensity, and are simply added to give an attitude score that places the respondent along the agreement/disagreement continuum of the attitude being considered. The measurement is to some extent contaminated, as some of the variation between attitude scores has been shown to result from such response habits as always choosing extreme positions on the scale.

Thurston's equal-appearing interval scale puts the attitude statements into an ordered set, and each statement is assigned a scale value:

Scale Value
1. I think this company treats its employees better than another company.   10
2. If I were starting again I would still join this company, etc.   8·5

The aim is to develop an interval scale, so that equal differences between overall (or average) scores represent equal amounts of change. Identical scores may reflect different patterns of attitude since the same score can arise from different sub-sets of statements.

A less commonly used scale is the cumulative, or Guttman, scale. It aims at measuring only one variable, so the result is an unidimensional scale.[1]

Whether any of these three are truly interval, or simply ordinal, scales, is a matter of controversy. The argument is that the inaccuracy resulting from treating them as such is more than compensated for by the gains made in the additional mathematical manipulation that is possible.

In evaluating employees, we may use
  (a) tests designed to assess aptitudes or theoretical knowledge about the job itself,

[1] See J. Guilford, *Psychometric Methods*, McGraw-Hill, New York, 1954.

(b) tests or results designed to show competence in performing the actual job itself, or

(c) some form of rating system.

Rating is a common method of 'measuring' an employee's performance. There are a number of systems but all suffer from inherent weaknesses.

1. *Order of merit systems.* Under this system, the supervisor arranges his subordinates in rank order, and a rating is given according to the subordinate's position in the rank. This is the 'rank order' method. An alternative system is known as the 'forced distribution' system, where subordinates are classified into categories according to the normal curve frequencies:

Lowest	Next	Middle	Next	Highest
10%	20%	40%	20%	10%

2. *Rating scales.* In an attempt to get absolute evaluation of an employee in terms of some criteria, various rating scales have been developed. The man-to-man rating scale was first used in the assessment of salesmen. For each characteristic on which a person is to be assessed, a common reference ('anchor') point is chosen— usually some person considered to possess a high amount of the characteristic. Others are rated against this reference point for their relative possession of the characteristic.

3. *Adjectival rating scales.* These scales employ lists of adjectives to cover extremes of the characteristic. Enough has been said on meaning to suggest the possibilities of differing interpretations for the adjectives employed. Hence, graded behavioural descriptive rating scales may be used to overcome the difficulty in interpreting adjectival scales. The supervisor ticks off those behavioural descriptions (often plotted along some scale) which most coincide with the employee's normal behaviour.

4. *The Q sort technique.* This is another rating method that tries to overcome the problem of the reluctance of raters to give unfavourable ratings. The rater is given a set of cards, each containing some descriptive phrase. He is then asked to sort the cards into categories from 'least like' to 'most like'. Instead of cards, the rater might be presented with some forced-choice rating scale containing similar adjectives, and asked to take those most like and least like the subject.

L

All rating systems have certain inherent dangers. One obvious defect is the failure to accumulate concrete evidence on which to base the rating, so that at worst the rating represents merely 'an unguided, subjective impression' that reflects 'nothing more than personal bias'. Among the more serious defects are the 'halo effect' and central tendency. The term 'halo effect' was first used by the psychologist Thorndike to refer to the fact that a single trait in which the individual excels or is manifestly inferior may cast a halo over other traits, so that the person rating may rate correspondingly high or low on other traits as well. Thus a person who shows willingness may undeservedly be rated high in output and quality. Similarly, a time study observer may award a high rating overall because the worker looks under stress ('putting his back into it'). The central tendency occurs, for example, in time study when there is a tendency to rate 'loose' at very low performances and 'tight' at very high ones. It may also arise from an unwillingness of the rater to rate. Fearing that such ratings may be used as an excuse for refusing a salary increase, the supervisor may deliberately award all his subordinates the same high rating.

The problem of getting out operational measures is more complex than has been indicated so far. Suppose, for example, we know the following about a sales supervisor:

Favourable	*Unfavourable*
1. Performance on Quota 90%	1. Known to tell his men that promotion based on 'who you know and not merit'.
2. Shows concern for his men in conversations with superiors. No evidence that subordinates find him other than considerate.	2. Neglects training and rationalizes with his superiors why training not necessary.
	3. Does not give his men a firm lead as indicated by the fact that violations of management policies continue.

Even if these generalizations were true, i.e. justified on the basis of the samples of behaviours collected, there would still be the problem of measuring their diverse consequences on a common scale that could be related to objectives. The connection between such behaviour and objectives is not given, and would require empirical investigation. The problem is not dissimilar to the evaluation of evidence. The connection between different forms of evidence (circumstantial, testimony) and the various rival hypotheses, is not clear, so that the weighting given to different evidence depends on judgment; we still use juries rather than computers to determine guilt.

RELATING OPERATIONAL MEASURES TO OBJECTIVES

Measures need to be tested for reliability and validity. Reliability is concerned with degree of consistency. In the field of testing, such consistency may take several forms:

1. Test/re-test reliability, as measured by the correlation between the results of taking the same test. Such a check reflects not only the lack of precision in the measuring device, but also lack of stability in the person measured in terms of the test.
2. Alternate form reliability, as measured by the correlation between two equivalent forms of the same test.
3. Internal consistency reliability, as measured by the correlation between two halves of the same test.

In areas other than testing, the emphasis is on consistency between the measures of various people. For example, if an employee rating system is developed, all raters should award the same grade in like circumstances, so the aim is to achieve inter-rater reliability.

As the validity of measures is concerned with the justification of inferences from scores, validity tests vary with the nature of the inferences to be drawn.

1. Predictive validity is checked by demonstrating that the measures help to predict future performance or events which could not otherwise be predicted.

   Usually the predictive validity of any single test is low. This is true even of IQ tests. Although they are the most important single instrument in testing scholastic aptitudes, the emotional overtones associated with the term 'intelligence' have given them a fascination out of proportion to their predictive validity.
2. Concurrent validity checks whether the measures distinguish

163

between groups already known to be different on the basis of other evidence, e.g. 'good' workers and 'poor' workers, as indicated by operator-performance indices.

For predictive purposes, a random sample of applicants should be recruited, and their subsequent performance on the job correlated to performance on the testing device. Such predictive validity is usually ruled out on practical grounds and resort is made to concurrent validity, where the assessed performance of current employees on the job is correlated to their performance on the selection device. Concurrent validity tests are less satisfactory as current employees have undergone training and cannot be regarded as a random sample of applicants.

3. Construct validity refers to the degree to which measures provide a basis for making inferences about the construct itself. What hypothetical constructs does this test measure which would account for the differences in performance on the test? Construct validity and validating a theory are intimately related.

   If an investigator insists that measures reflect a particular hypothetical construct, he needs to demonstrate construct validity by deducing and confirming consequences. For example, measures from a test must not only rank people, but the rankings themselves must be in accordance with predictions stemming from the background theory.

4. Content validity is demonstrated by defining the population of interest, and showing that the behaviour or test items are representative of it.

Validity checks on selection tests are often inadequate, making selection methods far from perfect. However (since the need is great) there are firms which, like marriage bureaux, promise a match that is currently beyond present techniques to achieve. But, as John Stuart Mill once said, 'Where it is impossible to obtain good tools, it is all the more important to know the defects of those you have.'

Chapter 11

PRESCRIPTIVE DECISION

THE RATIONALISTIC MODEL

Decision as a process should be distinguished from decision as a product; the latter is merely the terminal act that stems from the decision process. It is with the former that we are concerned in this chapter. The process of prescriptive decision involves a number of stages before the decision-maker selects from among the alternative courses of action:

1. Setting out the objectives to be pursued.
2. Discovering the relevant alternatives.
3. Ascertaining the consequences that will arise if a particular course of action is adopted, and discovering the relationships between selected courses of action and outcomes.
4. Evaluating outcomes into a 'payoff' in terms of the goals to be achieved.
5. The decision itself—the terminal act—that is likely to incorporate hidden influences, restrictions and values.

The above sequence is apt to hide the role played by the decision processes already discussed. The relevant alternatives depend on the sort of problem to be solved, so that the collection of data and the explanation of occurrences is often a prerequisite to the specification of alternatives. Also, the discovery of consequences is in the nature of prediction, while their evaluation often entails the sort of judgment issues discussed in the chapter on evaluation.

The emphasis in rationalistic decision-making lies in justifying action by following a rational process, as right thinking is an aid to right action. C. I. Lewis has pointed out that success cannot be guaranteed, so that to show that one's action is warranted by the evidence (given a specific goal) becomes of particular importance. In fact, it allows a superior to make a critical assessment of a subordinate's plans because the reasoning behind them is exposed. In general, a superior controls the plans made by subordinates by checking whether the goals are congruent with overall objectives, and the plans themselves feasible in terms of time and cost; the assessment of a plan's logical structure is often neglected.

In evaluating the past decisions of a manager, it is easy to look back and point to factors that were indicative of what was happening but which were seemingly ignored by the manager. But this is wrong if it ignores the other factors that indicated some opposite conclusion and for which the evidence was stronger at the time.

LAYING OUT OBJECTIVES

The course of action selected is intended to pursue some goals. This is often forgotten when experts indulge in futile debate over which is the absolute best method. For example, there is the debate over direct costing and absorption costing. Neither is undeniably the better; absorption costing may be better for company evaluation purposes, while direct costing may be better for other forms of decision-making.

To say that a course of action should further some goal is something more than saying that courses of action must be consistent with goals. Courses of action are always consistent with goals as long as they do not actually reduce goal attainment. Objectives can be put at such a high level of generality that most action can be shown to be consistent with them. Thus, both sides in a war can be said to have the same objective of peace. Additionally, individual efforts viewed separately may each even appear to contribute to goal attainment, but when examined collectively may be seen to be working at cross purposes to each other. Hence there is a need for co-ordination to establish that lower level goals do in reality further overall objectives.

Goals themselves serve as a means to higher goals and are judged by their contribution to these ends, as shown diagrammatically in Fig. 17.

Thus any goal can be shown to be an intermediate goal serving as a means to achieving some higher objective. On these grounds, goals are seldom 'sacred' if alternative means are available. As Rapoport points out,[1] 'So-called ends are often the results of an inadequate evaluation of the means available in the pursuit of basic ends'.

[1] Anatol Rapoport, *Operational Philosophy*, John Wiley & Sons Inc., New York, 1953, p. 126.

Goals are usually multiple and conflicting; in pursuing one goal, other goals are sacrificed or achievement of them is diminished, either because means are too scarce to achieve all ends or because achievement of all goals is logically inconsistent (e.g. act legally, and increase prices by monopolistic action). Seldom is any set of goals pursued single-mindedly; there are always constraints.

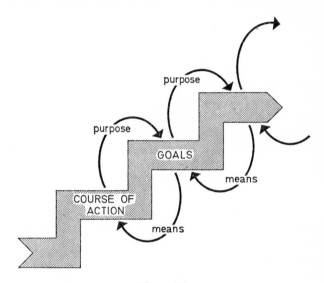

Figure 17

At each stage in goal attainment, there is the likelihood of changing direction to pursue other goals, in order to achieve an optimum mix. Goals may also be allocated a priority in time as well as resources. Thus the achievement of some company profit will usually take precedence over providing sports pavilions for workers but, at some profit level, social objectives which cannot be tied directly to long- or short-term profit goals may take precedence. Such goal substitution can be described in the language of marginal utility.

There are also natural constraints resulting from limitation of resources or of means legally acceptable. Certain other constraints are implicit. Thus, goals to meet some production target may specify cost and quality restraints, but may take for granted that the production manager will not get output at the expense of safety or

167

machine maintenance. Only where constraints might be violated are they likely to be stated explicitly.

This is not to suggest that staff should always take objectives as they are given. Objectives as given may not be in the best interests of the company, and should be queried where such doubt exists. They may be too narrow, perhaps concentrating on optimizing some sub-system (say, on achieving lowest production costs) which if achieved may be detrimental to the interests of the total system (say, by sacrificing flexibility needed to maintain adequate customer service).

Ackoff points out that all relevant objectives are seldom revealed through the usual form of questioning. He recommends as a supplementary procedure, confronting the decision-maker with each alternative and asking him if he would adopt the alternative if the proposed research results upheld it. A negative answer suggests the need for further probing to reveal the additional objectives not met by the proposal.[1]

IDENTIFYING ALTERNATIVES

Once aims are clarified and the problem has been explained and defined, then alternative courses of action need to be identified, unless appropriate action has already been established by precedent or policy.

Since the process of identifying courses of action determines what solutions are put forward for consideration, it is a factor in determining the quality of the decision finally taken; it is helped by the explanatory process which delineates the factors likely to affect the problem. Explanations of events clarify problems and direct the search for alternatives, and rule out a range of inappropriate ones. It follows that those holding different theories are likely to suggest different courses of action. For example, though both psychoanalysis and learning theory assume that neuroses stem from past experience affecting present conduct, psychoanalysis explains in terms of repressed memory and drives while learning theory explains in terms of faulty learning and conditioning. These different theories give rise to different courses of action as reflected in treatment.

In identifying courses of action we are identifying types, as each

[1] Russell L. Ackoff, *Scientific Method*, John Wiley & Sons Inc., New York, 1962, p. 71.

course of action can assume many forms. In designing an order handling system, the alternative solutions might revolve around, say, different machine systems (e.g. punched cards, offset litho, spirit duplicating, etc.), but each solution could take many varied forms.

Identifying alternatives can be a highly creative process, but it is given direction by an understanding of the system of which the problem is part.

Creativity is a mental process whereby some novel idea is produced that is regarded as useful in the solution of some problem. It is stimulated by accurate perception and memory, which help to fit together the relevant pieces of information, though often creative ideas may appear to arise without effort as if conjured up from the unconscious mind. Logic can be used to help choose between explanations and courses of action; it does not in itself originate them.

Creativity then is a psychological process but so far psychology has provided no techniques to guarantee the creation of ideas. However, there is some evidence that creativity can be stimulated, and the literature has been concerned with describing techniques that are claimed to achieve this, as well as with describing perceptual, intellectual, emotional and environmental blocks that diminish creativity. Among the main techniques described are simple ones such as these:

1. The use of check lists.
2. Attribute listing. Important characteristics of the product or process are listed, with the aim of changing them through free association, to fulfil new functions or to provide better functioning.
3. Brainstorming. People working on a problem are brought together to interact and stimulate each other into originating ideas. The imagination runs free, the aim being in the first instance to stimulate the quantity of ideas. Early criticism of them is discouraged, since premature criticism tends to inhibit the free flow of ideas.

IDENTIFYING CONSEQUENCES

There is a need to identify the likely consequences arising from alternative courses of action. These may be desirable or undesirable from the point of view of goal attainment. Goals form a criterion for selecting among alternatives or, more accurately, for choosing the alternative with the most favourable set of consequences.

Consequences can also be classified as immediate or long-term, and as probable or improbable. There is always a danger of ignoring undesirable side effects and long-term consequences, and of regarding improbable consequences as highly probable.

Some alternatives are automatically ruled out as being undesirable or not feasible. For instance, we may not be able to transfer labour elsewhere and past commitments may prevent us from making such labour redundant. Also, in examining the consequences of alternatives, there may be no need to list all relevant consequences; only the differential consequences among alternatives will be of interest.

Where each course of action is known to have some unique outcome (for example, where there is a causal relationship between action and effect), the decision is made under conditions of certainty. Where there are several sets of possible consequences attached to a course of action (for example, the different possible results from research expenditure) and the probability of any set occurring is known, then decision-making occurs under conditions of risk. Knight, the economist, also distinguished the situation where no probability could be attached to the different sets of possible results, which he referred to as decision-making under uncertainty. The distinction between the last two categories is usually ignored on the ground that decisions are never made under conditions of complete uncertainty or under conditions of precisely known risk.

Alternatives may not only have different sets of possible consequences attached to them, but each set may itself be split according to the effect on different groups. For example, a policy or law may have differential impact on the different groups to whom it applies. The fact that a policy or law is general does not imply that its impact is generally equal or fair, as it may discriminate in practice among groups.

Every course of action has certain inherent possible consequences, but these are not obvious. For example, what are the consequences of scheduling responsibilities? There is no strict causal chain to ensure it will reduce conflict in an organization by legalistically determining each person's function. In fact, it could be argued that such scheduling can lead to conflict, because it emphasizes individual assessment rather than team spirit. Both sets of consequences do arise in different circumstances or, more technically, under different states of nature.

The relationships between courses of action, states of nature, and outcomes, often need to be established by empirical inquiry. This is often forgotten; all too frequently management has many meetings to discuss some proposal under the mistaken belief that the racking of brains will produce the full set of consequences. In practice it merely leads to the exchange of ignorances and the postponement of the decision. Yet alternatives themselves do suggest consequences. Without knowledge of inherent potential it would not have been originally possible to regard the course of action as relevant to the problem.

Where models exist there is the opportunity for simulation to determine the effect of changing certain variables. Such manipulation of a model differs from mere trial and error, as the experimenter knows what is being changed, thus making simulation a less costly learning process while raising the possibility of establishing causal relationships.

There need be no direct relationships between action and result. Predicting consequences may require establishing the probability of various natural states occurring, and these might not be influenced by the course of action to be taken; this is as illustrated in the example below. Thus the sales of some products are influenced by the weather, so that selecting an amount to stock may require a prediction of weather conditions.

EVALUATING CONSEQUENCES AND FORMULATING DECISION RULES

There is a need to evaluate the consequences of the various courses of action. This raises a number of problems. There is first that of developing a criterion for evaluation. One general criterion is profitability, but it is difficult on occasions to make it operational. The second problem lies in assessing each consequence against the criterion. Thus one course of action may give lowest distribution costs, while another gives fastest delivery time. As already pointed out, there may be difficulty in making the comparison in money terms and hence in terms of profitability. The problem lies in the fact that the consequences are not of the same kind. To order

171

consequences we must be able to compare them, but this requires that the consequences belong to the same class. How do we transform a cost outcome scale into a delivery outcome time scale, or both into a common scale? We must know how to trade-off increases along the delivery time scale for increases along the distribution cost scale. For each incremental change, we might seek to measure the corresponding change in value and utility to the decision maker. Ackoff discusses the possibilities of doing this while detailing the various attempts to measure the relative value an individual places on objects, events or states.[1] An alternative approach is to seek to express the outcomes of the trade-offs in terms of the general objective of efficiency while leaving the decision-maker to allow for other values. Finally, Ackoff points out that optimizing behaviour may not be followed at all. It is common for the decision-maker to simply put forward a standard to be attained (e.g. diminish cost by fifty per cent) while laying down as a constraint some minimal level of acceptable performance elsewhere (e.g. quality of service not to be reduced).

A common approach, shown in Table 5, is merely to weight the relative importance of the differential consequences and then rate the alternatives from (say) 1 to 3 according to the relative amount of the consequences they are likely to produce. The rating multiplied by the weight would give the weighted rating of each consequence. The overall sum of the weighted ratings constitutes the overall assessment of the alternative. The alternative selected is that with the highest overall rating. Of course, such a linear weighting scheme has a large element of arbitrariness. Hence, it may be advisable to do some sensitivity analysis by changing different weights and ratings to gauge the effect.

The Payoff Matrix

An entirely different problem lies in discounting consequences in terms of their probability of occurrence. We will illustrate this with an example. A fashion shop manager can buy an article *XYZ* for £10 to sell at £15. At a maximum he might sell five, but he might not sell any. Thus, there are six states of nature representing the possible numbers demanded. These states form an exclusive and exhaustive set. Any stock unsold at the end of the season can be sold in the sale for £5 each item. The problem lies in determining the number

[1] Ibid.

Table 5. Evaluation of consequences of various alternatives

Differential Consequences	Criterion weight	Rating of alternatives				Points awarded alternatives			
		1	2	3	4	1	2	3	4
A. Competitive strength and market position	30	3	2	1	1	90	60	30	30
B. Ensuring sources of supply	20	3	1	1	1	60	20	20	20
C. Use of current distribution channels	5	1	1	3	1	5	5	15	5
D. Satisfying shareholders	10	1	2	2	3	10	20	20	30
E. Extent within marketing know-how of management	15	1	1	3	3	15	15	45	45
F. Extent within technical know-how of management	5	1	1	3	3	5	5	15	15
G. Extent to which labour skills and labour force remain same	5	1	2	3	3	5	10	15	15
H. Extent to which capital not needed	10	1	2	3	3	10	20	30	30
Totals						200	155	190	190

173

to stock. A 'payoff matrix' for the various courses of action is shown in Table 6. For example, if he buys 4 and sells 3 then the gross profit is £$(3 \times 15 + 5) - (4 \times 10)$ = £10.

If the retailer ignores any calculation of probability of demand his attitude alone will determine the number he buys. A pessimist expecting minimum profit or maximum loss will look down the action columns and select that course of action that gives him the maximum of the minimum payoffs, that is, he will use what is known as the *'maximin'* criterion.

Table 6. Payoff Matrix

		Course of action (number bought)					
		0	1	2	3	4	5
		£	£	£	£	£	£
State of	0	0	−5	−10	−15	−20	−25
nature	1	0	5	0	−5	−10	−15
(number	2	0	5	10	5	0	−5
demanded)	3	0	5	10	15	10	5
	4	0	5	10	15	20	15
	5	0	5	10	15	20	25

The minimum profit of maximum loss of each course of action is:

Action	Worst outcome
0	0
1	−5
2	−10
3	−15
4	−20
5	−25

All the above outcomes are the expected outcomes for each of the possible courses of action from the pessimist's point of view. Hence he will select a course of action which gives him 'the best of a bad lot', i.e. the maximum of these minimum payoffs which is £0 for action 0.

If the retailer were an optimist he would look down the action columns and select the maximum of the maximum payoffs. This is the *'maximax'* criterion.

The maximum profit of each course of action is:

Action	Best outcome
0	0
1	5
2	10
3	15
4	20
5	25

As the above outcomes are the expected ones for each course of action, the optimist will select the best of these, i.e. the maximum of the maximum payoffs. This would be action 5 which gives the maximum payoff of £25.

One further decision rule would be to look down each action column and select the minimum of the maximum payoffs. These are the same as before:

Action	Best outcome
0	0
1	5
2	10
3	15
4	20
5	25

The person midway between optimist and pessimist may select the course of action which is the minimum of these maximum payoffs. This again would be action 0 giving the payoff of £0. This is the 'minimax' criterion.

Another alternative is expected profit. It assumes in this case that the probability of each state of nature (amount demanded) can be estimated. Where a situation is repetitive, it may be possible to calculate objective probabilities from the relative frequency with which one or more similar items have been sold in past years. Otherwise, recourse is made to subjective probabilities, where the decision-maker relies on his judgment. The calculation of subjective probabilities shares many of the characteristics of rating. The decision-maker tends to over-estimate the occurrence of those events with a low objective likelihood of occurrence, and to under-estimate those events with a high objective probability of occurrence. One suggestion to improve the calculation of subjective probabilities is to ask the decision-maker if he would prefer either to get a prize if the state of nature did occur as predicted, or to take part in a raffle for the same prize in which he had a proportion of the tickets equal to the probability P he had assigned to the state of nature. The decision-maker should regard the two as giving the same probability P of winning the prize. However, if he should make the first choice, his estimate of probability is likely to be too low. If he makes the second choice, his estimate is likely to be too high.

Table 7

(1) *Payoff for action* 4	(2) *Probability*	(3) *Col.* (1) × *Col.* (2)
£		£
−20	0·02	−0·4
−10	0·10	−1·0
0	0·20	0·0
10	0·40	4·0
20	0·20	4·0
20	0·08	1·6
	Expected profit	8·2

To return to our example. Suppose the retailer's calculation of probability was as follows:

Number demanded	*Probability*
0	0·02
1	0·10
2	0·20
3	0·40
4	0·20
5	0·08
Total	1·00

The probabilities add up to 1, because it is assumed that the number demanded is certain to fall between 0 and 5. They are multiplied by the appropriate payoff in the action column, and then the products are added. Thus the expected profit for the fashion season for action 4 is calculated in Table 7.

The calculated profit for each action is shown below. Action 3 yields the highest expected profit and would be the course of action selected.

176

Action	Expected profit
	£
0	0
1	4·8
2	8·6
3	10·4
4	8·2
5	4·0

On the assumption of perfect information, profit would be higher. Thus buying at £10 and selling at £15 would give the following profit for each amount bought:

Amount bought	Profit
	£
0	0
1	5
2	10
3	15
4	20
5	25

Assuming that the amounts bought are in accordance with the probabilities given, then profit per day would be

$$£(0·02 \times 0) + (0·1 \times 5) + (0·2 \times 10) + (0·4 \times 15) + (0·2 \times 20)$$
$$+ (0·08 \times 25) = £12·7.$$

Since in the absence of perfect information the highest profit is £10·4, perfect information would increase profits by £12·7−10·4 = £2·3 a day. It follows that it would be worth paying up to £2·3 a day to obtain perfect information.

Where there is some considerable doubt about a particular subjective probability, various other estimates of probability can be tried to gauge the effect on the payoff matrix and thus on the decision. In this way estimates of probability are revised to measure the *sensitivity* of the decision to changes in probability.

The management scientist and researcher may help the manager,

(a) in drawing up the list of exclusive and exhaustive states of nature;
(b) in weighing the evidence to reach the probabilities to be attached to the various hypothetical states of nature, and
(c) in drawing up the various courses of action.

M

DECISION TREES

Decisions give rise to other decisions. A decision tree, that proceeds by showing the chain of alternating action and outcome, is one way of laying out such a problem. Thus one set of actions and outcomes may be represented as in Fig. 18.

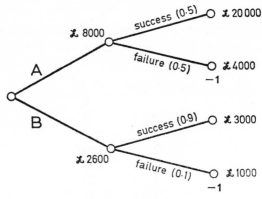

Figure 18

This decision tree indicates that if we produce A we have a 50% chance of making £20,000 and a 50% chance of losing £4,000. The expected value is therefore

$$£(0·5) (20,000)+(0·5)(-4,000) = £8,000.$$

Similarly, if we produce B we have a 90% chance of making £3,000 and a 10% chance of losing £1,000. The expected net value is therefore

$$£(0·9) (3,000)+(0·1)(-1,000) = £2,600.$$

The evidence would suggest that we produce A in preference to B on the ground that, if this decision were made many times and assuming the probabilities are correct, A would give an average profit of £8,000 as against B's £2,600. But the decision may be a 'one off' as far as the decision-maker is concerned. In any case he may still prefer a 90% chance of making £3,000 with only a 10% risk of losing £1,000, to a 50% chance of making £20,000 but with a 50% chance of also losing £4,000. The repercussions arising from error (e.g. capital loss) may be such that the manager chooses other

178

than to maximize expected profit. The best course of action may not be the selection of maximum expected profit when there is a risk element involved. Hence, it could be argued, the differences in probabilities neither reflect the risk the manager is willing to undertake nor should undertake in the light of circumstances.

There are ways of incorporating into decision procedures an allowance for the decision-maker's attitude towards risk.[1] For example, in the illustration below, the range of outcomes was from − £4,000 to £20,000. The problem is to obtain a rule of correspondence to transform any point along such a range into a measurement

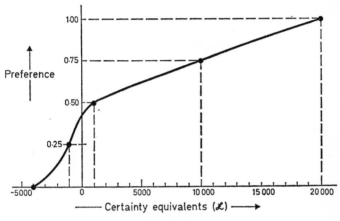

Figure 19

of attitude towards risk. We can plot the range of outcomes along the horizontal axis, and a corresponding measurement from 0 to 1 along the vertical axis (Fig. 19).

The decision-maker can choose either a fifty-fifty gamble on winning £20,000 or losing £4,000, or he can receive a certain sum of money. The sum of money is adjusted until he is indifferent towards the two alternatives. This sum of money is the so-called 'certainty equivalent' of the gamble. If the answer is £1,000 then £1,000 is the certainty equivalent to the gamble proposed. As the gamble covered the two extremes of the range it would fall midway on the vertical preference scale 0 to 1. Thus the (x, y) plot is (1,000,

[1] R. Schlaifer, *Analysis of Decisions Under Uncertainty*, McGraw-Hill, New York, 1969.

179

0·5). Similarly, if the decision-maker were given a fifty-fifty chance of gaining £1,000 or of losing £4,000, the corresponding certainty equivalent would have a preference measure of 0·25. We will assume his certainty equivalent is −£1,000. Finally, if given a fifty-fifty chance of winning £20,000 or winning £1,000, the decision-maker might choose a certainty equivalent of £10,000 to correspond to a preference of 0·75.

The money values in our illustration can now be converted into the preference measures:

Money values	Preference
£20,000	1·00
− £4,000	0·00
£3,000	0·55
− £1,000	0·25

The calculations are as follows:

$$(0·5)(1·00) + (0·5)(0) = 0·5,$$
$$(0·9)(0·55) + (0·1)(0·25) = 0·52.$$

Consequently the expected preference for A is 5, while that for B is 0·52. Hence, taking into account the decision-maker's attitude to risk, the choice is changed from the production of A to the production of B.

CRITICISM OF THE RATIONALISTIC MODEL

The rationalistic model of prescriptive decision-making as described above has been subject to a number of criticisms, on the grounds that the model is both unrealistic and undesirable once the limited abilities of the decision-maker are taken into account.[1]

We have discussed the problem of evaluation. Few of the examples quoted would fall readily into a payoff matrix approach, which assumes knowledge of probability distributions over the states of nature, though the data banks in most companies may offer no real basis for allocating probabilities to outcomes. The initial use of subjective probabilities, subsequently improved through the Bayesian inference process, may appear to be a solution. But the procedure may have limited usefulness, when much decision-making consists

[1] David Braybrooke and Charles E. Lindblom, *A Strategy of Decision*, The Free Press, New York, 1963.

of estimating continuous streams of joint probabilities of statistically interdependent events. New combinations of events demand new estimates, not (as in Bayes) revised estimates of old combinations. Yet we have no way of estimating joint probability from individual events when these are statistically interdependent.

The payoff matrix also assumed that the consequences or outcomes of alternatives can be measured on a common scale and that the scale can be a ratio scale. Such is not always possible. There can never be any guarantee that all the relevant alternatives have been identified. Herbert Simon points out that, in any case, decision-makers do not explore all alternatives but end their search once a satisfactory solution has been discovered; the decision-maker's behaviour is 'satisficing' rather than maximizing. Similarly, cost and time restraints rule out his finding all consequences through pilot runs, simulation and so on. Charles Ramond illustrates the problem dramatically:

'Given just the dozen marketing activities mentioned above, and five levels of effort that could be applied in each, he could choose among 5^{12} or roughly 238 million possible allocations.'[1]

On these grounds the rationalistic decision-making procedure has been regarded as undesirable in that, if taken seriously, it would lead the decision-maker into the futile search for the best technical solution and waste his energies, since 'even the second best solution comes too late, and the best never comes at all'. It is wrong to reject an alternative if it is the best available simply on the grounds that it is not the best conceivable; that which is most desirable may not be the most feasible. This criticism is perhaps unfair since running through all discussions on the rationalistic model is the concept of efficiency and value of information. We are warned at every stage to consider whether additional search for information could be justified in terms of its effect on results. But alternatives are often infinite once the possibilities are also considered. Thus there may be only twenty known ways of processing an order, but each of these ways has a great number of forms it could take. The rationalistic model takes final goals as given. It gives no guidance on goal formation, and it is essentially concerned with economizing on means to achieve given ends.

[1] Charles K. Ramond, *The Limits of Science in Marketing*, unpublished MS, Graduate School of Business, Columbia University, p. 23.

But such an emphasis is wrongly placed for many types of decision. Diesing points out that if the aim of the decision is effectiveness in carrying out group action, the emphasis should be on achieving an integrated group.[1] The concept of economizing has little relevance in this context. Similarly, legalistic decisions aim to stabilize conflict rather than to economize on means. In fact the rationalistic model makes the implicit assumption that the participants to the decision share common goals and evaluative criteria. This is seldom realistic. Decision-making invariably has political elements, where the emphasis is on reaching some agreement through the processes of persuasion, bargaining or straight exercises of power.

[1] Paul Diesing, *Reason in Society*, University of Illinois Press, Urbana, Ill., 1962.

Chapter 12

AN OVERALL VIEW

The manager in his decision-making must interpret, classify, describe, explain, evaluate and predict. However, he is distinguished from the scientist in several ways. In the first place, there is an emphasis on evaluation and, most of all, on prescription—two processes that involve value judgments. In the second place, he, like the historian, is a consumer and not a producer of 'laws' or other explanatory systems of wide generality.[1] Generalizations he must make to understand and analyse the problem; all the better if these generalizations are borrowed from the findings of science rather than 'common-sense'. The manager, though, does not himself collect data to establish general truths, but general truths are used to determine which data are appropriate are the problem solution.

All this is not to deny that every managerial problem has unique features; all problems do. It does not follow from this that treating certain problems as belonging to a class of problems, and thus amenable to a certain type of treatment, is impossible. In fact, it is essential and the only way to interpret what is meant by experience.

If the solution of even everyday business problems is facilitated by the guidelines embodied in the processes of scientific inquiry, then these should be part of a curriculum in business studies. There is recognition of this, and business schools are placing less emphasis on committing facts to memory and more emphasis on research methodology, decision-making techniques and model-building. But this is still too narrow. It represents a too restricted interpretation of the scientific method. There is an emphasis on techniques and tools rather than the broader aspects of methodology. Thus, we find that the mathematical model is put forward as if it were the only acceptable explanatory framework, regardless of purpose or the nature of the problem. Such processes as description and

---

[1] G. H. Nadel (ed.) *Studies in the Philosophy of History*, Harper Textbooks, Harper & Row, New York, 1965.

evaluation receive little formal treatment. Of course, this may be the inevitable result of forgetting that these processes depend on underlying theories and concepts, and of classifying them as aids to explanation rather than forms of explanation in their own right; a classification that serves the purposes of exposition but may be dysfunctional to the purpose of distributing the right amount of emphasis in problem-solving. There is also the whole problem of

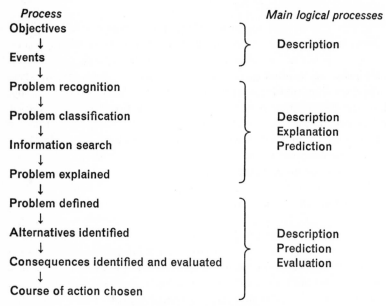

Figure 20. *Prescriptive Decision*

the nature of evidence and 'proof'; too few research papers in social science give it the attention it deserves.

The steps in decision-making, as usually described, are limited to setting objectives, seeking alternatives and consequences and making a choice from among these consequences. Such a contraction of the decision-making process may lead the manager to neglect certain crucial elements. A more realistic model might consider decision-making as involving description, explanation, prediction and evaluation. The output from these processes can be regarded as decisions in themselves though, more commonly, they would be regarded as sub-processes to the prescriptive decision (see Fig. 20).

We might illustrate this process by even the simplest of examples. A manager may note an increase in absenteeism in one department. He assumes this to be a problem by recalling that the plant is fully employed so that absent workers will lead to loss of output and profit. He classifies the problem vaguely as a 'personnel problem' and seeks information from the personnel manager and the plant supervisor. Both put forward tentative explanations. The personnel manager is particularly convincing with his hypothesis that the absenteeism is the result of new work methods and points out research findings that support the relationship between work dissatisfaction and absenteeism. On investigating, this seems likely since the absenteeism did occur from the date the new methods were introduced. Furthermore, the workers, when questioned, expressed an unfavourable attitude towards the new methods. The hypothesis of the plant manager—that lax supervision is the reason—seems unlikely since the rise in absenteeism is of sudden growth while supervision has not been changed. Alternative solutions to the problem are put forward (return to old methods, offer a financial incentive to those with low absenteeism, some compromise between the old and new methods that would satisfy the workers without sacrificing all the potential of the new method) and their likely consequences discussed. In discussing consequences, both research findings (e.g. that a settlement via participation will cause least dissatisfaction) and experience (e.g. that incentives for non-absenteeism will be demanded by other groups in the factory) are drawn on. These consequences are evaluated in terms of what is best long-term for the company. The decision is to select the solution that is most congruent with these objectives.

All decisions presuppose an objective and an event is recognized as potentially giving rise to a problem when it is seen as a threat to objectives or as a means to enhance objectives. But problem recognition involves aspects of description, namely, observation and perception and a hypothesis that there is a problem. It is not unknown for a manager to believe he has a problem when, in reality, he has misinterpreted the event, e.g. a request for union recognition as a sign of impending labour militancy.

As a manager recognizes a potential problem, he seeks to classify it. There is a danger of the specialist having a predisposition to classify most problems as coming within his particular field of competence. Thus, constant late deliveries might be classified by the

O.R. specialist as an inventory control problem, by the systems and procedures specialist as an order-handling problem, by the industrial psychologist as one of personnel selection, by the organization expert as a co-ordination problem, by the social psychologist or sociologist as a problem in group motivation, and so on. The problem may be amenable to just one of these approaches or to several or to none of them. As the manager classifies a problem, he is stating that the solution falls within some field of knowledge and is, therefore, setting up some hypothesis that requires testing.

The classification of the problem determines the tentative solution without which no progress can be made. The tentative solution determines the information search so that a problem clearly falling within some particular field of competence is one where the information search is guided by the system of relationships among the factors of which the field is composed. Every statement of a problem asks about relationships between elements in a system and the tentative solution suggests how the various elements might be interrelated. The more a system is understood, the more selective is the information search. The less understood the system (e.g. in marketing), the more speculative and wide ranging is the search for factors that might have some relevance to the problem. Hence, at the stage of information search the manager draws on explanations based on either his own experience or the work of others. If he tests his hypothesis, he seeks to corroborate some set of predicted consequences and to confirm that the hypothesis is consistent with other known facts.

Information has a data base in observation and testimony (Fig. 21). If the data base is erroneous, subsequent processing may also lead to erroneous descriptive statements. The testimony we seek and what we observe (whether directly or indirectly by way of records), is guided by a criterion of relevance determined by the tentative solution, i.e. how the manager believes the problem can be solved. But testimony needs corroboration; observation involves interpretation and data from both sources are classified, defined and recorded in language which can symbolize something other than what was intended. The manager's perception or interpretation of some observation or testimony depends on the concepts and attitudes built up from his experience. This can give rise to error and unconscious bias which may not be conducive to the purpose at hand. The interpretation of behaviour at interviews is an obvious

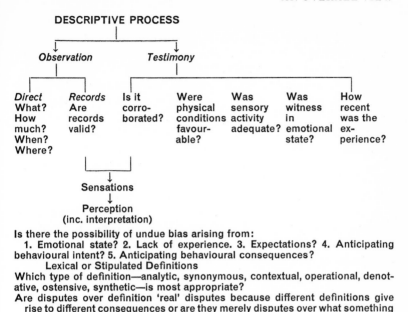

DESCRIPTIVE PROCESS

Observation   *Testimony*

Direct	*Records*	Is it	Were	Was	Was	How
What?	Are	corro-	physical	sensory	witness	recent
How	records	borated?	conditions	activity	in	was the
much?	valid?		favour-	adequate?	emotional	ex-
When?			able?		state?	perience?
Where?						

Sensations
↓
Perception
(inc. interpretation)

Is there the possibility of undue bias arising from:
1. Emotional state? 2. Lack of experience. 3. Expectations? 4. Anticipating behavioural intent? 5. Anticipating behavioural consequences?

Lexical or Stipulated Definitions
Which type of definition—analytic, synonymous, contextual, operational, denotative, ostensive, synthetic—is most appropriate?
Are disputes over definition 'real' disputes because different definitions give rise to different consequences or are they merely disputes over what something should be called?
↓
Classification and Division
Has the most suitable genus and basis been selected for the purpose?
Are the categories exhaustive and mutually exclusive?
↓
Expression in Language
Have the symbolic overtones of the language been considered?
Has emotive language been avoided if description is to be factual?
Has the danger of reification been avoided?
Have words been changed (e.g. titles) in belief that reality now changed?
Does the language conjure up false analogies that could mislead?
Has the two-valued orientation been avoided?
If the statement is a definition of the problem, has it been stated operationally for it to be solved empirically?
Is proof being demanded for statements that are merely extensions of definition?
Is the statement significant in that, if true, it would affect the decision?

Figure 21. *The Process of Description*

example where the interviewer's perceptions may be warped by (say) class bias.

Interpretation involves classification, but such classification may not be the one formally adopted once the purpose of the classification is established. Whether the process is one of division where a class (genus or sub-set) is broken down into sub-classes (species or sub-sets), or of classification where the process is one of grouping into classes, the procedure depends on having concepts about how the sub-classes may be related. Even a classification of accounting records reflects a specific purpose and its development requires knowledge of the subject matter of accounting.

Perceptions are expressed in language, and language helps mould perceptions while perception guides the selection of language. But words symbolize different things to different people and affect them differently. The words used, therefore, to describe a situation can themselves be a factor in affecting the solution. Thus, the salesman is taught to say that clients are 'owning' not 'buying' certificates and are making an 'investment' rather than a 'payment', as the choice of words can affect buying action.

A statement, though, should not merely be expressed in language carrying the 'right' symbolic reference but should be useful to the purpose, testable if put forward as an hypothesis and, if true, with consequences for the decision. There is little point in wrestling with problems about what might have been or in being diverted into issues where the establishment of truth or otherwise is irrelevant to the problem.

Throughout the decision-making process, assumptions are accepted because they seem to be reasonable. This is inevitable; time demands make it impossible to check all assumptions. Yet a mental review of assumptions being made is a useful exercise as some are better treated as hypotheses and put forward for testing. One of the advantages of the 'outsider' (consultant or newly appointed executive) is that he is more likely to question what others take to be axiomatic. A mental test of an hypothesis would take the form of testing it on several counts—its coherence with other known 'truths'; whether it seems to relate the facts in a manner that 'makes sense'—and attempting to deduce consequences which, if true, would appear significant to its truth. Finally, there would be a deliberate attempt to set up rival hypotheses which, when similarly tested, can be rejected if less likely or accepted if more likely. Of course, there is a limit to what can be achieved by mere intelligent self-reflection (e.g. some consequences can only be confirmed by experiment) but time is apt to rule out more controlled empirical approaches (Fig. 22).

A problem explained is a problem diagnosed. But an explanation can take a number of forms. In general, to repeat Nagel, an explanation may describe the conditions under which the event to be explained varies or fits into some known system or follows from some principle accepted as true. More specifically, an explanation can simply be a valid deduction from some 'law', theory or model or a probable conclusion from a statistical generalization or an experiment establishing functional relationships of a probabilistic nature (Figs 23–7). Sometimes the manager may speak of 'finding the cause'. But cause is an elusive concept; the scientist would prefer the less theory-loaded concept of 'functional relationship'.

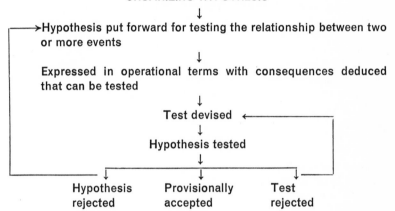

ORGANIZING HYPOTHESIS

1. Does hypothesis explain the situation to be explained?
2. Does hypothesis cohere with other known 'truths'?
3. Have consequences been confirmed?
4. Are consequences deduced and confirmed multiple and surprising?
5. Has significance of confirmed consequences been assessed for truth or falsity of hypothesis e.g. negative evidence of little significance?
6. Have rival hypotheses been eliminated or simplicity principle applied?

Figure 22. *The Process of Hypothesis Testing*

Yet at the macro-level, it is still inevitably used, though just what antecedents are selected as the cause varies with purpose. In management, those antecedents selected that are 'actionable' are labelled 'cause'.

Another category of explanation is that which takes the form of a genetic explanation that first determines the forces at work and traces their interactions from some point in history to show the

189

LAWS

↓

Hypothesis explaining kinds of events that survives the test of time and testing

↓

Shown to be a universal proposition related to other such propositions within a system

↓

Accepted tentatively as law expressing functional or causal relationship

↓

1. Does the law explain *kinds* of events as it should?
2. What antecedents does it link to what consequents?
3. Are antecedents merely occasioning conditions or pre-conditions or some of both?
4. Is term 'cause' being used appropriately?
   (a) At macro-qualitative level?
   (b) Suitable for the purpose, e.g. in management as referring to those abnormal conditions that are actionable?
   (c) Not too general or far back?
5. If interacting system, which (cause or effect) is actionable?
6. Has the danger been avoided of confusing cause with mere antecedent or mere association of events whose co-existence results from common cause?
7. Is it clear which causal conditions are being sought—necessary, sufficient, contributory or contingent?
   ∴ Has alleged cause been corroborated?
   (a) Consequences confirmed or failure explained?
   (b) Rival hypotheses refuted or have less simplicity?
8. Have we avoided believing that cause and effect must be of the same nature?
9. If experimentation adopted, has analysis of variance been used to take account of effects varying in degree, operation of chance and effect of several factors in producing results?
10. To what populations can results be generalized?
11. If experimentation with people
    (a) Have matched groups been used to allow for changes occurring due to time and contemporaneous events?
    (b) Has 'placebo' been given to control group to allow for experimental process effects?
    (c) Have additional control groups been used to allow for effect of some initial measure of pre-experimental state?
12. Where interrogation used, has procedure been carried out to avoid questionnaire, interviewer and interviewee bias?
13. Does the corroboration depend on the acceptance of attributes of hypothetical constructs that remain uncorroborated?

Figure 23. *The Formulation of Laws*

necessary conditions leading to the present problematic situation (Fig. 28). Still another type of explanation is the teleological one, (Fig. 29). One variation of this is where the antecedent 'causal condition' takes the form of 'motive for doing'. Motives are usually regarded as a necessary condition for action and are accepted as explanations because they go beyond the immediate observed

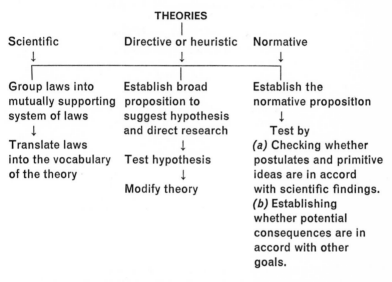

THEORIES

Scientific	Directive or heuristic	Normative
Group laws into mutually supporting system of laws	Establish broad proposition to suggest hypothesis and direct research	Establish the normative proposition
Translate laws into the vocabulary of the theory	Test hypothesis	Test by *(a)* Checking whether postulates and primitive ideas are in accord with scientific findings. *(b)* Establishing whether potential consequences are in accord with other goals.
	Modify theory	

1. Does the theory interrelate laws so that evidence for the truth of one law provides evidence for the truth of the others?
2. Is the theory a system of laws or simply a heuristic device to give direction to research?
3. Is the uncorroborated heuristic theory being used as support for some hypothesis?

Figure 24. *Theory Formation*

behaviour. The other type of teleological explanation is the functional which stresses the contribution or function which some sub-system plays in maintaining or attaining the goals of the total system. Function implies system and role within a system and so is distinguished from mere effect. However, functional explanations do, in a sense, simply reverse the cause and effect sequence. But a full-blown functional explanation does more because it shows how the

191

structure of the system changes, the degree to which goals are attained by the contribution of the system's parts and how the parts themselves interact to bring this about.

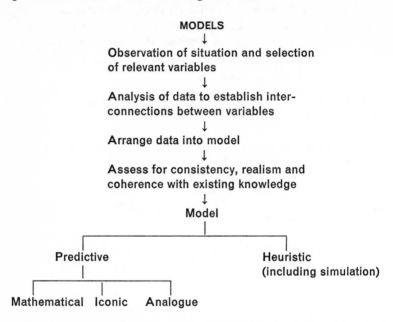

MODELS
↓
Observation of situation and selection of relevant variables
↓
Analysis of data to establish interconnections between variables
↓
Arrange data into model
↓
Assess for consistency, realism and coherence with existing knowledge
↓
Model

Predictive   Heuristic (including simulation)

Mathematical   Iconic   Analogue

1. Does the model possess internal consistency while avoiding over-simplification, false analogy or unjustified metaphor?
2. Should the model be isomorphic for the purpose?
3. Which approach is most appropriate—from simple to realistic model or complex to simple manageable model?
4. Are necessary variables missing?
5. Are unnecessary variables present?
6. Are numerical values assigned to the variables correct?
7. Are the functional relationships correctly specified?

Figure 25. *The Development of Models*

The level and type of explanation most appropriate will differ with the problem, even though explanations are often interrelated and may differ merely in emphasis. Consider, for example, the situation where there is dissatisfaction with a wage payment system. The manager may note that identical grades of labour do not receive the same basic wage. He may be familiar with some research findings that show that wage differentials for the same type of job are the main source of dissatisfaction with pay. He explains the current situation in these terms:

1. All wage differentials for the same type of job are cases that give rise to dissatisfaction with pay.
2. The current situation is one where there are wage differentials for the same type of job.
3. Therefore, the current situation is one that gives rise to dissatisfaction with pay.

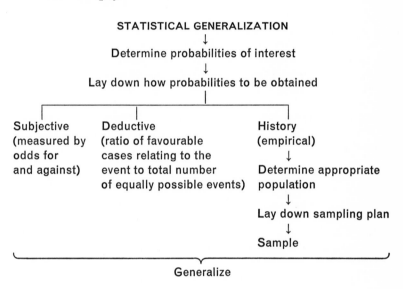

STATISTICAL GENERALIZATION
↓
Determine probabilities of interest
↓
Lay down how probabilities to be obtained

Subjective (measured by odds for and against)	Deductive (ratio of favourable cases relating to the event to total number of equally possible events)	History (empirical)

History (empirical)
↓
Determine appropriate population
↓
Lay down sampling plan
↓
Sample

Generalize

1. Is the generalization suggestive of explanation?
2. Has the correct population been selected?
3. Is the sampling-plan well designed?
4. Are the mathematical manipulations suitable for the scales being used?
5. Have the measurements been checked for reliability and validity?

Figure 26. *The Process of Statistical Generalization*

Alternatively, he may go into the history of the problem to see how current wage payment systems evolved to reach the present state. He may even suspect that the real source of dissatisfaction is not wages but something else. He seeks other motives and, to determine the workers' perceptions of the situation, questions them on the grounds that any solution must take their perceptions into account. Again, he may note that the wage demand was occasioned by the installation of financial incentives in another department

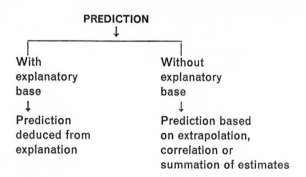

1. Can the Bayesian inference process help to improve initial subjective probabilities?
2. Is the prediction likely to be a self-fulfilling prophecy or a suicidal one?
3. If the prediction is purely deductive, is the deduction formally valid?
4. If the predictive process lacks an explanatory base, has the process been tested for past success?
5. If the predictive process entails explanation, have its assumptions been verified?
6. What background constants are assumed to persist?
7. What trends are expected to continue?
8. What assumptions are made about the actions of others?
9. What inherent consequences of alternatives are assumed.
10. How are other consequences derived?
11. Have legislative as well as empirical consequences been considered?

Figure 27. *The Process of Prediction*

having the same grade of labour. He may regard this as the cause and offer to install financial incentives instead of giving an increase in basic pay. Finally, he might analyse the role that wage demands play in the system of interpersonal relationships between management and men; how a failure to negotiate in a way that is perceived as fair and reasonable reduces the goodwill that is an output from the system. There may be no long-term victory if one partner in a symbiotic relationship feels humiliated by the other. A total view of the situation might consider all these approaches and test each tentative solution, though in practice, habit, attitude, and ignorance of the explanatory process lead the decision-maker to concentrate on just one.

An explanation does give direction and help in identifying more precisely the appropriate alternatives. But alternatives themselves

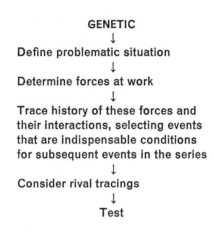

GENETIC
↓
Define problematic situation
↓
Determine forces at work
↓
Trace history of these forces and
their interactions, selecting events
that are indispensable conditions
for subsequent events in the series
↓
Consider rival tracings
↓
Test

1. Does explanation show 'how possibly' the problem has evolved by tracing interrelationships between past, necessary causal antecedents from previous period T to the current problematic situation C?
2. Have the 'facts' been corroborated?
3. Are the assumptions justified?

Figure 28. *The Genetic Explanation*

have consequences which must be determined. Although alternatives have certain inherent potential, predicting relevant consequences is not always just a matter of inference. The relationship between alternative courses of action and their consequences forms the subject matter of much empirical and scientific inquiry. What are the conditions under which action A will produce effect B? Some intended consequences do not arise because (say) other forces were at work while unintended ones do arise. However, if a solution follows from a valid explanation, the risk of putting in a solution

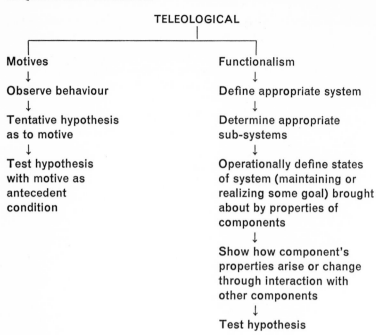

TELEOLOGICAL

Motives	Functionalism
↓	↓
Observe behaviour	Define appropriate system
↓	↓
Tentative hypothesis as to motive	Determine appropriate sub-systems
↓	↓
Test hypothesis with motive as antecedent condition	Operationally define states of system (maintaining or realizing some goal) brought about by properties of components
	↓
	Show how component's properties arise or change through interaction with other components
	↓
	Test hypothesis

1. Is motive merely justifying reason without validation of motive construct?
2. Is assumption of motivated state justified?
3. Is the assumption being made that establishment of motives establishes fact?
4. Is assumption being made of the single motive or that different cultures have the same motives?

1. Is function performed by some component a contributory, necessary or sufficient condition for emergence of certain properties of the system?
2. Has appropriate system been defined?
3. Are there operational criteria to indicate the various states of the system brought about by the properties of its components?
4. Can some other component perform the function?
5. Have the state of the components themselves been explained.

Figure 29. *The Teleological Explanation*

that does not produce the intended effects is reduced, though we may still be faced with undesirable side effects because of a failure to gauge the impact of consequences on the total system.

A major problem lies in evaluating consequences (Fig. 30). The assumption that a money value can be placed on consequences in an explicit manner restricts the application of the payoff matrix,

EVALUATION
↓
Establish objectives and
measures of objectives (criteria)
↓
Determine relevant attributes
to be evaluated
↓
Determine operational definitions and
measures of attributes
↓
Relate operational measures to objectives
and establish validity
↓

1. Are the criteria an intermediary objective?
2. If so to what extent are criteria related to ultimate objectives?
3. Are the rankings on the criteria reliable?
    (a) Are the criteria ambiguous?
    (b) Is performance on the criteria to be subjectively assessed?
    (c) Do the criteria presuppose set conditions which may not materialize?
    (d) Have users of criteria the same concept of standard?
4. Are the measures made by measurement instruments reliable and valid?
5. Can consequences be put in form of a payoff matrix?

Figure 30. *The Process of Evaluation*

though it is a useful concept none the less. Evaluation of consequences in relation to goals is still generally a matter for executive judgment. We have no scientific way of weighing up different kinds of evidence or of gauging, for many problems, the effect on objectives of increments of one consequence against increments of another if these consequences are of a different nature.

To sum up, the line manager is concerned with prescriptive

decision-making. This process, however, involves the more scientific processes of description, explanation and prediction and the judgmental elements involved in evaluation. It is these additional processes that have been neglected in courses formally dealing with decision-making. It is training in these processes that would remedy a serious deficiency.

Index of Proper Names

199